The 3-day diet

Choose whichever 3 days suit you best ... super-flexy!

To our beautiful husbands and children who have to listen to our relentless healthy-eating lectures. Thank you for encouraging us and loving us ... along with our weird avocado-choc-broccoli experiments!

Also heartfelt thanks to the thousands of SuperFastDiet members who bare their souls to us every day – it is such a privilege to share in your life-changing transformations. It's why we do what we do ... we LOVE you!!!

We advise that the information contained in this book does not negate personal responsibility on the part of the reader for their own health and safety. It is recommended that individually tailored advice is sought from your healthcare or medical professional. The publishers and their respective employees, agents and authors are not liable for injuries or damage occasioned to any person as a result of reading or following the information contained in this book.

Victoria Black & Gen Davidson

Pan Macmillan Australia

Contents

Let's play 'Have you ever?' 6
The birth of SuperFastDiet 8
Meet the easiest diet ever 13
What you'll learn in this book 15

The nuts and bolts of the 3-day diet 17

Meet the future you 35

Supercharging the 3-day diet 45

The one where they finally talk about food 53

Enjoy the things that make life worth living 69

Mindset 101: strategies to supersize your success 83

Contents

CHAPTER 7

The recipes 105

Staples 109

200 CALORIE BREAKFASTS
117

300 CALORIE LUNCHES
133

400 CALORIE DINNERS
147

100 CALORIE SNACKS & DRINKS
203

100 CALORIE DESSERTS
217

FAQs 230
Where to from here? 232
Thank you 233
Conversion chart 234
Index 235

Let's play 'Have you ever?'

This isn't your ordinary weight-loss book. Which is just fine and dandy, because you're not an ordinary human, are you? You're a glorious, sparkly superhuman who's about to become even more super. We created this book for champions like you, who, for whatever reason, just can't seem to slay the scales. But we're going to do it together *and* it's going to be loads more fun and way easier than you ever thought possible.

Let's start with a game ...

- ☐ Have you ever failed at a diet?
- ☐ Have you ever done well on a diet for a while and then failed?
- ☐ Have you ever lost weight and then put it back on again?

We've been there. Believe us, we tried for years to lose weight. Sometimes we'd even succeed, but we'd always end up right back where we started. But you know what, it's not you, it's those diets.

Scientists have proven that not only are most diets ineffective, they're also unsustainable long term. There are a stack of studies proving that continuous daily calorie restriction is almost impossible to stick to, no matter how great your motivation is or how strong your willpower. And something else they don't tell you is that if you do it for too long; it can even damage your metabolism. Yep, the very method you're using to make you healthier might actually make you *unhealthier* in the long run. Our research also revealed that extensive exercise isn't that great for weight loss either. But this diet's different. It's easy. And it's sustainable in the long term.

Okay, next question.

- ☐ Have you ever hankered after a glass of wine?

Yes? What about cheese? Chocolate? French fries? Us too! We love food! And that's the real difference between this diet and others: it won't ask you to be 'good' all the time, because that's unsustainable. It won't even ask you to be good half of the time. All it asks is that you be good three days a week – just three! And even then you don't have to be 100 per cent perfect, just clever. (We'll teach you how.)

- ☐ Have you ever been sick of dieting?
- ☐ Have you ever worked your butt off without any results?
- ☐ Have you ever struggled to find motivation?
- ☐ Have you ever been so B.O.R.E.D. of eating bland fish and limp-looking carrots that you're almost ready to poke your own eyeballs out?

Okay, then. How would you like to be able to choose *what* you eat, and *when* you eat? How would you like to still be able to eat ice cream and cheese and chocolate and ALSO lose weight? It sounds too good to be true, right? But it's not.

- Have you ever wanted to lose weight easily and effortlessly and keep it off forever?
- Have you ever wanted to keep off that weight but still be able to go out and have a glass of wine and a cheese plate with your friends?

Well, we have good news: it's possible. It's ALL possible. Seriously! And we're going to show you how.

But before we do, three quick things ...

1 We wrote this book for you!

Our goal (obviously) is to help you lose weight. But we're a little more ambitious than just that. This book is designed to become the first step in a better life for YOU. We'll help you lose weight, but we'll also help you do it sustainably and for the long term. That doesn't mean the weight loss will be slow (in fact, it's likely to be the opposite), but it *does mean* that not every single step will immediately make sense as a 'weight-loss thing to do'. Some of what we're going to teach you is about mindset, some is probably better defined as 'lifeset', some is simply designed to help you become the person you were always meant to be. And some of it is just for funzies.

2 We'll be asking you to do a little bit of work (not much!)

Many authors write books about themselves and tell *their* stories. But we're here to talk about you. That means that there will be a little bit of work required on your part. Some of this will require you to look inside yourself for answers, some will require you to look outwards, some will ask you to look back, but mostly we'll be asking you to look forward and to move forward. Inside this book, you'll find to-do lists, step-by-step instructions and activities that will help you lose weight, but also help you to get happy, be healthy and generally become even more awesome than you ever thought possible.

3 We're going to keep it short and sweet (promise)

We won't be feeding you any poppycock in these pages. No empty promises. Just the tools and the information you need to kick those kilos forever and kick off a SuperLife in the process. It's time to get excited! This is the first step in a much bigger journey to becoming your best self. But first, rosé. No, wait, it's only Tuesday. Coffee then.

The birth of SuperFastDiet

Ever noticed how the people who are meant to be in your life always end up gravitating back towards you, no matter how far apart you wander or what strange paths life takes you down? We have! The two of us became friends in the early 1980s, a time of neon Lycra, black spandex, G-string leotards, epic perms, Barbie-pink fingernails and vertigo-inducing stilettos. In those days, we were working for Gloria Marshall Figure Salons, an American chain of weight-loss centres peddling outrageous exercise equipment such as 'The Roller' (aka the 'fat jiggling machine'), which would revolve around our kneeling clients, slapping their tummies and thighs into submission in order to uncover slenderer physiques hiding within – or at least that was the promise.

Back then, the weight-loss industry was bizarre and the diets so ridiculous that even the most motivated of women would end up hungry enough to eat an elephant. Nevertheless, we loved every second of our jobs. Motivating other women, talking about health and fitness ... it all felt very natural to both of us. We were two twenty-something sasspots doing exactly what we were meant to be doing. But even so, we couldn't shake the feeling that something was wrong with the system we were selling. We suspected that if we really set our minds to it, we could do so much better.

In fact, we daydreamed about creating our own weight-loss program one day. We'd brainstorm ideas and come up with marketing campaigns, but there was something missing – something critical: a holistic weight-loss program that worked in the long term. We had the sense that the right idea was sitting there, just out of our peripheral vision, but no matter how hard we tried, we couldn't bring it into focus. At least, not yet.

Both of us had always been relatively slim. And while we were working in weight loss, well, let's just say we had plenty of motivation to choke down sad little 80s salads and greyish portions of steamed fish. But as we 'grew up', we got married, started new careers (Vic went into marketing and magazine publishing while Gen set up a chain of gyms). We had kids and began using ice cream and wine to cope with work stress, lack of sleep, disobedient children and ... well, basically, life happened, and we got fat. And not the happy 'jolly Santa Claus' type of fat. Sad fat. We got sweet-baby-cheeses-and-holy-guacamole-on-toast-how-the-heck-did-we-let-it-get-this-bad fat. We missed our spunky slender selves.

Both of us were fed up and desperate to get back to our former glory, and we gave nearly every method out there a go, racking up thousands of dollars on gym memberships, personal trainers and every stupid diet out there!

You name it, we were on it. The Israeli Army Diet, the eggplant diet, the lemon detox diet, the South Beach diet, juice cleanses, the baby food diet, charcoal detoxes, eating dessert with breakfast and that one crazy diet where we had to wear blue-tinted glasses anytime we ate anything (IDK why). We tried the stuff that everyone else tried, but it didn't work for us – not in the long term.

Throughout all these ups and downs we kept in touch because we loved each other's company and had a shared passion for personal development. Catching up also gave us the perfect opportunity to cry into our cappuccinos about how yet another dieting attempt had ended in a giant mushroom cloud of, 'Ahh, bugger it. This isn't working anyway.'

That was until a certain lunch date in 2015 changed everything

Vic: Oh, yes! I remember that lunch date well. Gen waltzed into that café looking like Little Miss Radiant in her skinny pants. Jaw on the floor, I gestured wildly to her dramatically slimmer form and said, 'Umm, excuse me! What's going on here?'

Smiling, she examined her perfectly manicured fingernails and replied ever-so casually, 'Oh, yahhh. Like, I *toootally* solved the whole weight-loss thing.'

Gen: I remember that lunch date, too. Vic couldn't get the questions out fast enough. She was all, 'So? What's going on? Did you finally crack it?! How are you so skinny?! Speak, dammit!'

I told her I was trying this new thing that I'd been doing a bunch of research on, and that I thought it might be the answer. So of course Vic grabbed my arm and said, 'THE answer?' When I nodded, she leaned back in her seat and looked at me with a mixture of disbelief and amazement. 'Holy snap, crackle and pop!'

And just what was this weight-loss miracle I'd discovered, you ask? Intermittent fasting (or IF for short). A way of eating (or not eating) that allows you to lose weight effectively and sustainably while also eating and drinking all the things you love. Boom!

While Vic stared at me, wide-eyed, I talked her through the simple IF routine I'd been following. It was called 5:2 because five days a week I ate normally, and the other two days I reduced my intake to 500 calories. I told her that once I got through the first two weeks of adjusting to this new way of eating, I was up and running! I ended up losing a whopping 30 kilos, which I've kept off in the years since. No wonder Vic's jaw was on the floor.

Vic: About a nanosecond after that fateful lunch, I hopped onto the IF bandwagon, raring to go! I tried the 2-day method first, which I loved, and then I also tested a part-day fasting method, where I fasted for the first part of each day and ate my first meal around lunchtime – making eight hours a day my 'eating hours'. If that plan sounds easy, it's because it was! Ten stubborn kilos that had been holding on for dear life finally started melting away, and within weeks I felt like my old bubbly, positive self again, only this time in smaller jeans! And all while still eating out and drinking wine with my besties when I felt like it. We'd finally found 'the answer' we'd been searching for. #nailedit

Fast forward through an epic movie montage of us both researching everything about IF we could get our hands on, phoning scientists and flying across the world to meet with university professors, writing in our notebooks, drinking mugs of cold black coffee and falling asleep on a big pile of books with our glasses all crooked (in this particular montage we both wear glasses).

As the evidence piled up all around us, we realised we were hurtling a million miles an hour towards that decades-old dream of creating our own weight-loss program. Driven by our desire to make weight loss as easy and as un-intimidating as possible, we created three different weight-loss programs, each centred around a different fasting method to suit different lifestyles, including our 3-day method. We made our programs, recipes, tips and content as fun, flexible and simple to follow as possible so we could support people on what we knew was a revolutionary and life-changing weight-loss journey.

In 2018, we realised our dream and launched our SuperFastDiet programs, website and community. Since launching SuperFastDiet, we've won countless awards, including the Optus MyBusiness Start-up Business of the Year, and our online program has exploded in popularity with members easily and consistently losing massive amounts of weight. But without a doubt, the most rewarding thing has been seeing the incredible transformations that so many members have experienced since joining us.

As most people who have shed a significant amount of weight will tell you, weight loss has the power to totally transform the way you see yourself and what you believe is possible for your life. Suddenly, the world feels full of possibilities. You've managed to slay this hard thing, so what other things might you be able to tackle? The magic starts when you believe in yourself.

Go online get your BONUS Secret Chapter at superfastdiet.com/3daydietbook

Meet the easiest diet ever

At SuperFastDiet HQ, we'd been referring to the 3-day diet as the 'Mary-Anne diet'. We named it after Gen's sister, who repeatedly told us she could never follow our other fasting programs because they were (in her words) 'too hard'. We were determined to find something Mary-Anne could do effortlessly, and the 3-day diet turned out to be the magic bullet. On this plan, she would 'fast' for three non-consecutive days of the week (eating only 1000 calories a day) and then eat normally during the other days. Well, Mary-Anne took to this diet like a duck to water, shedding an impressive 25 kilos and sailing to her goal weight of 63 kilos just in time to dance the night away on her 50th birthday in an age-inappropriate miniskirt. These days she says she feels 10 years younger, and we reckon she looks it too!

Right before launching SuperFastDiet, we decided to include the 3-day diet as one of our methods. It was, quite honestly, an afterthought, so imagine our surprise when, post-launch, we discovered that thousands of our members agreed with Mary-Anne; they also found the 3-day diet the easiest of our methods by far. Not only were they achieving short-term results that were just as impressive as members on our other two methods, they were also finding this diet sustainable in the long term.

It was clear to us that people loved this diet and that it was working for all types of people, bodies and lifestyles. While discussing this diet one day, we both came to the realisation that nobody had written a book on a 3-day diet quite like this before. It was time!

We popped our imaginary glasses back on and got to work researching. We wanted to make sure that what we were recommending was 100 per cent the most effective, simple, sustainable method of weight loss available. Our research led us to Krista Varady, Ph.D., Associate Professor of Nutrition at the University of Illinois, Chicago, and one of the world's leading researchers of IF as it relates to weight loss.

> 'I think this method is so effective because there's no counting carbs, avoiding entire food groups or expensive meal replacements. It's simple, it allows flexibility, it makes you feel good! It also works quickly, helps to improve your health, and it allows you to maintain your weight loss long term.' – Krista Varady, Ph.D.

What is intermittent fasting?

The scientifically agreed-upon definition of IF is 'periods of eating, followed by periods of not eating'. Essentially, it's an eating approach that encourages you to delay rather than deny. And this is one of the keys to its success, both in terms of its sustainability and its long-term effectiveness.

Intermittent fasting is an umbrella term that collectively describes several different eating approaches. These include the alternate daily fasting (ADF) approach pioneered by Varady, where you dramatically restrict calories every other day of the week, and then eat normally on the other days; the popular 5:2 method where you eat normally for 5 days, and fast or dramatically restrict calories for 2 days; time-restricted feeding (also known as 'part-day fasting' or '16:8') where you only eat during certain hours of the day; and 'one meal a day' (OMAD).

A surprising scientific discovery

Professor Varady was so excited that someone had finally decided to write a book about this method, because she'd come to a similar conclusion as us about the 3-day diet. After years spent researching a method of ADF where participants were eating 500 calories on their fasting days, Varady accidentally discovered that people who were eating 1000 calories on their fasting days rather than 500 found the diet more sustainable and, therefore, more effective than the method she'd been researching.

You see, her clinical trial group was set up to follow a regime where they would fast for two days a week, eating no more than 500 calories on those two fasting days. But the group couldn't stick to that plan. They were cheating on their diet and consuming 1000 calories rather than 500 (sneaky little suckers) on their fast days. But despite their cheating, the members of the trial group consistently lost weight. In response, the research team switched them to the method they'd been sneakily following for the next six months of the survey. Turned out the method the trial group had accidentally created worked even better than the original!

Now we were even more convinced that we'd found the weight-loss holy grail. What choice did we have but to share it?

What you'll learn in this book

We've got so much good stuff for you coming up in the next few chapters. Here's some of what you'll learn.

- How to lose weight without counting calories every day.
- How to lose weight easily and effortlessly.
- How to maximise your fat-burning power and minimise the calories you take in, *without* feeling miserable. In fact, most of the time, you won't even notice you're on a diet.
- How to flip that magic fat-burning switch in your body and the skinny-person switch in your brain, which will allow you to burn fat while you're sleeping, while you're eating, while you're having your hair done and even while you're online shopping (talk about living the dream).
- The ins and outs of the 3-day diet – a little-known fasting method that will not only blow your wobbly bits away, it will blow your mind. Once you learn about this method, you're going to want to share it with everyone. And we highly encourage you to do just that.

We're not in this just to sell a million books (though, obviously, if you suggest to your friends that they buy this book, that would be awesome!), we're in this to make lives better and longer and more 'super-er'. We want you to try this 3-day diet because we're sure you'll love it, we know you'll see results and we're willing to bet you'll find following it simpler than you could have ever imagined IF to be.

You'll learn about some very simple methods that will make weight loss doable, easy and freaking fun. There are plenty of tactics in these pages as well: 'how-to' approaches that will help you implement the methods easily, as well as give you the tools, the timelines and the techniques to turn them into a routine, which will very quickly become a habit. Something you couldn't fail at even *if you tried*. We're here to make sure you never have to diet again. Ever. Promise.

So, here it is: the 3-day diet. We hope it changes your life the way it has changed the lives of thousands of our members.

P.S. We've organised a super-special free trial of our award-winning online SuperFastDiet program especially for you. Head over here to collect it! superfastdiet.com/3daydietbook

CHAPTER 1

The nuts and bolts of the 3-day diet

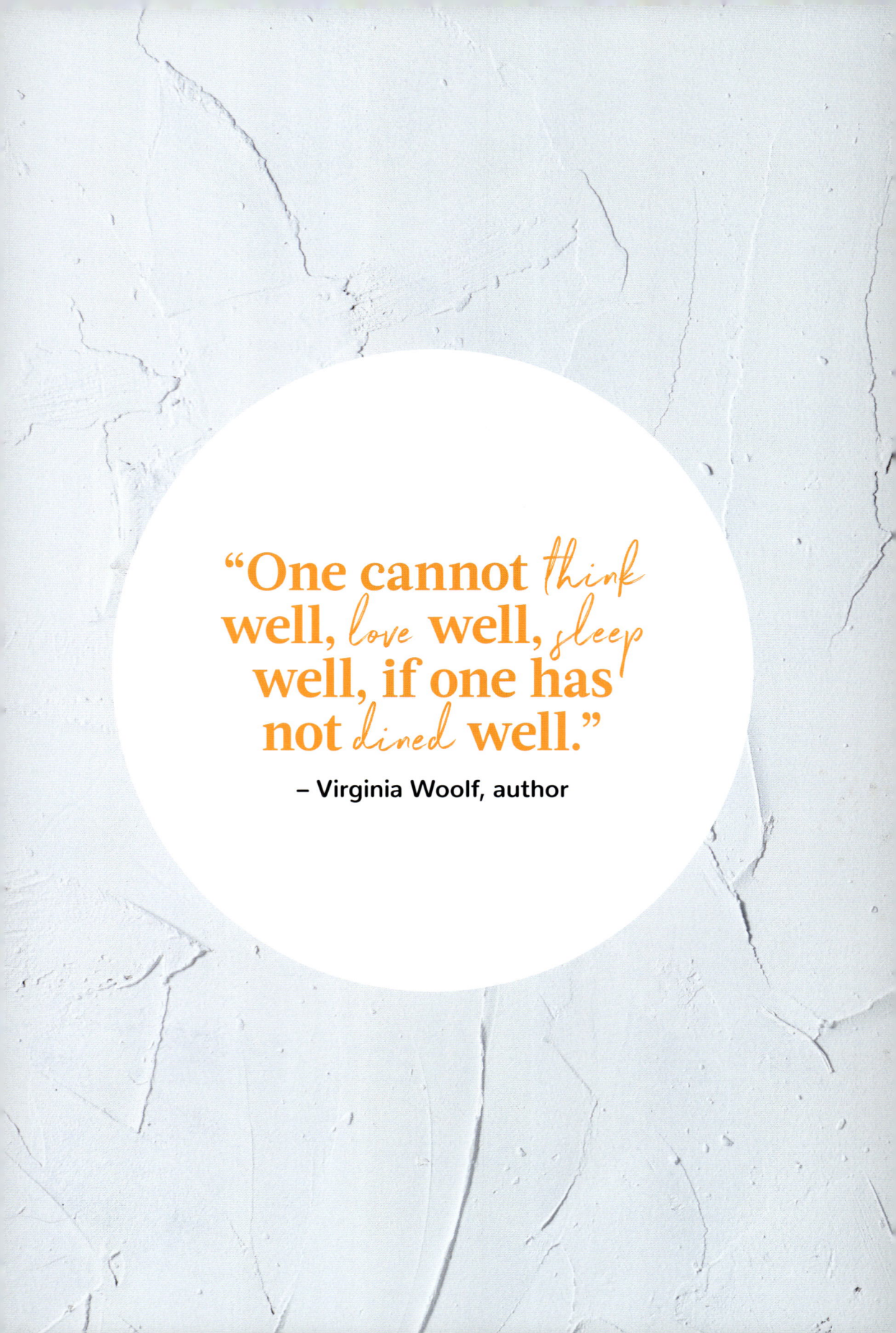

"One cannot *think* well, *love* well, *sleep* well, if one has not *dined* well."

– Virginia Woolf, author

The anti-diet

We honestly thought about calling this book *The Anti-Diet* because the words 'fasting' and 'diet' tend to conjure up images of deprivation, sad little salads, being forbidden from eating anything remotely enjoyable and going to bed at 4 pm. Granted, that strategy *can* work, but it can also make you miserable because (say it with us) food is awesome! Food is life. WE. LOVE. FOOD.

But here's the great news: the 3-day diet is currently one of the easiest IF methods available. To the point where we're *almost* stretching the definition of IF (almost). You don't have to give up the food or wine you love in order to achieve your weight-loss goals. Because while this diet does fall under the umbrella term of IF, we prefer to call this method 'part-time dieting' because it's a diet that you only need to follow *part* of the time – on your 'on days'. The rest of the week you're enjoying 'off days' where you can eat, drink, be merry and still lose weight. Score!

The beauty of this approach is that for every 'on day' you do – where you stick to a calorie count and do the hard yards – you're rewarded with an 'off day'. That makes this diet ideal for people who:

- struggle with hunger
- find it difficult to cut calories or restrict their calorie intake
- love breakfast
- exercise regularly and, therefore, find themselves hungrier throughout the day.

> Alexa, play 'Celebration' by Kool & The Gang, we're ready for a dance party!

Top 10 reasons why the 3-day diet is awesome

1 It's incredibly effective for weight loss.

2 You won't feel as hungry as you do on other diets.

3 It helps you burn body fat by inducing ketosis.

4 It helps trim belly fat.

5 It's particularly effective for women in menopause.

6 It keeps the body's metabolism running high.

7 It helps maintain muscle mass.

 It is a lot less restrictive than other weight-loss methods.

 It's easy to stick to.

 It's very sustainable long term.

Each one of these claims is backed up by cold, hard science. And the great thing about IF is that it has a truckload of health benefits that other diets can't touch (more on these on page 22). And when you follow the 3-day diet method, you get all the weight-loss and health benefits of IF, *without* having to do all the hard bits. Sneaky, huh?

> Intermittent fasting is scientifically proven!

The 3-Day Diet

15 bad-ass bonus health benefits of the 3-day diet

There's a reason IF is one of the A-list's secrets to getting (and staying) lean. Celebrities love part-time dieting because it doesn't just give them a bangin' J-Lo or Chris Hemsworth-style bod, it also makes them look younger, feel more energetic and smack down a whole host of diseases including diabetes, cancer, Alzheimer's and Parkinson's disease. That's right! The 3-day diet is so much more than just a weight-loss miracle. It's also an anti-aging, cancer-fighting, inflammation-soothing bonafide health-bestowing phenomenon. Don't believe us? Stand back, we're about to drop some knowledge.

1 Lowers bad cholesterol
LDL cholesterol levels (the 'bad' cholesterol that marks the increased risk of cardiovascular disease) decrease by 10–20 per cent.

2 Increases good cholesterol
HDL cholesterol levels (the 'good' cholesterol that marks a decreased risk of cardiovascular disease) increase by 10–15 per cent.

3 Lowers blood pressure
IF lowers blood pressure levels by 5–10 mm Hg, which reduces the risk of heart disease.

4 Increases your enjoyment of food
Studies have found that your taste receptors and sense of smell are increased when you do this diet, meaning you enjoy even simple foods more.

5 Decreases cravings
A recent study found that fasting on alternate days resulted in a decreased preference for high-energy, calorically dense foods.

6 Helps you feel younger and healthier
All the extra good foods in our recipes and meal plans are going to give you more vitamins, which means healthier skin and hair, plus a renewed zest for life!

7 Reduces belly fat
Waist circumference has been shown to decrease by 5–7 cm. This is the dangerous visceral fat that can cause a lot of health problems!

8 Lowers insulin resistance
IF reduces insulin resistance by 20–40 per cent, which assists in lowering the risk of type 2 diabetes.

9 Reduces inflammation
Studies show that inflammation markers such as TNF-alpha and IL-6, which are linked to heart disease and diabetes, are reduced during fasting.

10 Slows the aging process and reduces the risk of age-related diseases
Can extend lifespan and promote healthier aging by reducing the biomarkers for aging, heart disease, cancer and diabetes.

11 Protects the brain
IF helps to protect neurons and allows them to better cope with stress and resist disease.

12 May prevent Alzheimer's
Helps improve neural connections in the hippocampus and protect neurons against amyloid plaques – proteins prevalent in those with Alzheimer's disease.

13 May prevent cancer
Reduces insulin-like growth factor 1 (IGF-1) by up to 50 per cent. IGF-1 promotes the growth of cancer cells, so by decreasing IGF-1 levels, scientists believe it may reduce your cancer risk.

14 Improves mood
Researchers have found that brain-derived neurotrophic factor (BDNF), which is produced when you fast helps improve mood, reduce stress and even lowers anxiety and depression.

15 Increases motivation
BDNF strengthens neural connections and increases neuroplasticity, which in turn can treat everything from low mood to chronic pain, helping you feel more energised and happier.

And let's not forget about autophagy!

Perhaps one of the biggest benefits of IF is that depriving your body of energy for a while turns on 'autophagy', which is essentially the body's clean-up process. During autophagy, the body clears away any old, damaged or worn-out cells to make way for shiny, new ones that work like a charm. Think of it like a refresh for your cells. A brand new you, from the inside out.

Isn't it amazing how the simple act of intermittent fasting can create a snowball effect in your body and your brain? How many other diets can claim a list of health benefits that epic? It's true that losing weight on another plan would also lower the risk of health complications, such as diabetes, cardiovascular disease and high blood pressure, but a diet that also helps prevent cancer, improves mood, reduces aging and makes you feel and look younger? Sign us up for that one! (Especially if we only need to follow it three days a week!)

The 3-day diet in three easy steps

Step 1: Find your magic number

First things first, you'll need to know your total daily energy expenditure (or TDEE). That's the number of calories (or energy) you burn in a day as your body goes about its business. Broadly speaking, your TDEE is the number of calories you need to consume in a day to fuel your body.

There are a few different ways of calculating TDEE using weight, height, age, gender and activity level. We use the Mifflin-St. Jeor equation, as it's popular among nutrition professionals and has been validated by various studies. And, according to the American Dietetic Association, it's also the most accurate way of estimating daily energy expenditure to within 10 per cent.

 Go online for the free TDEE calculator on our website to get your magic number. superfastdiet.com/3daydietbook

Step 2: Choose your 'on days' and 'off days'

The 3-day diet is proven to be just as effective as the other methods in our SuperFastDiet program, but even more generous and more sustainable thanks to the flexibility and freedom it offers. To succeed with this method, you just need to follow these guidelines each week:

Choose three days to be your 'on days'

Eat 1000 calories per day (or 50 per cent of your TDEE). Typically, Monday, Wednesday and Friday are good 'on days'. But you can choose any three days you like. It's great to have an 'off day' in between an 'on day' if you can, but it's not necessary.

On your 'off days', live your life as normal!

Eat 2000 calories per day (or 100 per cent of your TDEE). Tuesday, Thursday, Saturday and Sunday are popular 'off days', but again, it doesn't matter. Choose the days that suit your life each week.

Step 3: How to break up your calories across the day

It might not sound like much, but 1000 calories is actually a stack of food if you know how to make it work for you. Considering most diets recommend restricting calories to between 1000 and 1400 calories every single day, it's easy to see why people find the 3-day diet so effortless and so sustainable. For every 'on day', you get a day off. How good is that?

The first column below shows how we suggest you break those 1000 calories up during the day. Alternatively, you may prefer to skip brekkie and roll those 200 calories into a larger lunch or a couple more snacks. It's up to you. If your TDEE is lower than 2000 and your fast days are more like 800 calories, refer to the second column to show how we suggest you break them up.

50% TDEE = 1000 CALORIES		50% TDEE = 800 CALORIES	
BREAKFAST	= 200 calories	BREAKFAST	= 150 calories
LUNCH	= 300 calories	LUNCH	= 200 calories
DINNER	= 400 calories	DINNER	= 350 calories
SNACKS	= 100 calories	SNACKS	= 100 calories
TOTAL	**= 1000 CALORIES**	**TOTAL**	**= 800 CALORIES**

Could this be the most balanced and sustainable eating plan ever?

Yes! We think so. To answer this question, let's first look at what makes a diet unsustainable. The way we see it, any plan that forces you to cut entire food groups out of your diet, such as carbs or dairy, or indulgences like alcohol or sugar are bound to be unsustainable in the long term. Other diets are unsustainable because they require you to constantly purchase frozen or delivery meals. How can you stick to a diet if you can't afford the meals? What if you need to go away for a few days? Or go out one night?! Before you know it, diet blown!

The beauty of the 3-day diet is that it doesn't require you to buy anything, cut out any foods or stop socialising. There are no powders, pills, frozen meals, crazy workout routines or complicated calculations. All you need to do is follow the method we've laid out for you and you'll lose weight sustainably and easily for the long term, in a way that's well balanced for both your physical and mental health.

On the four days a week that you aren't dieting, continue eating in a normal, healthy way, and enjoying those date nights, birthday parties and weekend barbecues that make life worth living! And because you can always get a day off after an on-day, you'll find you're less likely to want to cheat on your diet. And if you do, that doesn't matter. You just move your 'on day' and make today an 'off day'.

Will this diet still work if I'm 'on' for less than three days a week?

Nope! Three is the magic number. The reason this is a 3-day diet and not a 1- or 2-day diet is because three days on and four days off is what studies have proven to be the most effective means of weight loss. Stick to the plan and follow the science.

Time to dismantle the rumour mill

Rumours and myths are rife when it comes to weight loss and what constitutes being 'healthy'. Mainly because a lot of people can't be bothered doing the research to find out what's fact and what's fiction, and because a lot of the media (and, disturbingly, some of what we'd consider the 'health industry') is surprisingly intertwined and/or controlled by peeps who have a vested interest in selling us food. (We're looking at you, large multi-national cereal corporations.)

It's very easy to get the public to immediately discount a diet if you term it a fad. Granted, many diets ARE fads. And many fads are diets. However, although it's controversial, IF (part-time dieting) definitely isn't a fad. It is backed by strong scientific and medical evidence, and many studies have now proven the benefits of it, yet there are so many misconceptions.

We've rounded up all of the current available scientific evidence on the effectiveness of this method for you. If you'd like to go and read the studies, which, by the way, is something we highly encourage you to do – everyone should learn how to read scientific studies so that they can verify health recommendations and scientific claims themselves – you'll find the studies that correspond to each section at superfastdiet.com. But for now, to set your mind at ease, let's call balderdash on one of the biggest myths out there.

Intermittent fasting will make you burn muscle

People who poo-poo intermittent fasting and part-time dieting like to talk about how not eating for long periods of the day will cause the body to go into 'starvation mode', which in turn will result in your metabolism slowing down, eventually causing you to 'burn muscle' for fuel. Well, that's a crock and here's why. All of us fast intermittently when we sleep. But we don't wake up with less muscle than we went to bed with. If we burned muscle every time we slept (aka when we are fasting intermittently) we'd be dead or unable to stand up at the very least.

Muscle is actually a terrible source of energy for our body; fat is far better. This is why our bodies burn stored fat for energy while we're asleep – that's what it's there for. Think about it: why would your body store energy as fat, but then burn muscle when it needed energy? That doesn't make any sense. Your body is smart. It stores energy as fat, and when it needs energy, it goes and gets those stores from … body fat.

Recent studies have shown that IF actually allows people to HOLD ON TO muscle mass far better than diets that require calorie restriction every day.

DIET TYPE	FAT LOSS	MUSCLE LOSS
Calorie restriction	75%	25%
Intermittent fasting	90%	10%

Studies have also shown that when you fast intermittently your levels of human growth hormone (HGH) increase almost fivefold, thereby helping you to build muscle mass as well as boost your ability to metabolise sugar and fat. The minute you start to research these criticisms about IF being a fad, burning muscle or causing starvation mode, they very quickly fall apart.

Meet Kristen

BEFORE: 77 kg **AFTER:** 63 kg   **KILOS GONE** 14 kg

Like many people, Kristen found stricter methods like 5:2 difficult to stick to. When she embraced the easier approach of the 3-day diet, she found that not only could she lose weight effortlessly, but she could do it with a glass of wine in one hand. Two years later and 14 kilos lighter, she has a renewed zest for life and feels ten years younger.

AFTER

BEFORE

'I was uncomfortable in my clothes, I felt sluggish and my confidence was low. I'd been invited to Hawaii for my sister's 50th birthday, and being my first overseas holiday – to a bucket list destination – I wanted to be happy in my own skin and feel comfortable in a swimsuit. By the time I was on the plane, I was 14 kilos lighter! I gave stricter methods a go, but found I would often blow out those 500-calorie fast days. So, I tried the 3-day diet. Well, it was fantastic! I now supercharge by pairing the 3-day diet with the 16:8. The 3-day diet is great, no expensive pre-packaged foods, no shakes, no supplements, no ridiculous fitness regimes and, most importantly, it is affordable.'

How this method gives you an MWA (Massive Weight loss Advantage)

Rather than struggling to stick to a difficult diet, we're willing to bet that you find that you breeze through the weeks on the 3-day diet. Numerous studies show that participants generally find this method exceptionally easy to stick to, which means it produces superior adherence levels. This is because it's a lot less restrictive than other diets. On top of that, study participants also report that they:

- feel less hungry and more satisfied
- enjoy food more
- burn more fat
- don't feel deprived
- feel their cravings are reduced
- are less likely to reach for junk food
- feel more inclined to exercise.

Basically, this method allows you to easily burn fat without even trying too hard. No more flogging yourself at the gym, no more starving yourself. Eat what you like on your 'off days', follow our 1000 calorie meal guide on your 'on days' and hey, presto! You'll be shimmying into your old jeans before you know it.

Can you really have your cake and eat it too?

YES! You really don't have to choose between eating yummy food OR being your ideal weight. You can do both. Our method is built around zero guilt. If you want chocolate, have chocolate. If you want French fries, eat 'em. If you want a glass of wine, drink the wine! Enjoying food is one of the greatest pleasures of life. Hooray!

Our favourite swaps #NoGuilt

We're not going to nag you about vitamins and minerals and why you need fibre and vegetables and protein. You'll get there eventually. Right now, the most important thing is that you learn a little bit about how to maximise calories on those all-important 'on days' and start to recognise how common little missteps can trip you up big time. Our goal is to make you self-sufficient, so to that end, here are a few of our favourite food swaps.

As you can see, the table opposite illustrates that the 'healthy' option isn't always the best for your waistline. Sometimes, too much of a good thing can stop you from slaying those scales. Keep in mind, this isn't about making food 'good' or 'bad'. Food is just food. We humans are the ones who attach meaning to it. How you perceive it, what you do with it and how much you consume of it is what makes all the difference.

A lot of us aren't aware of the caloric differences between many of the choices we make. Who would've thought that eating a wholewheat cracker instead of a piece of toast could save you more than 100 calories? And how many of us would guess that enjoying a few pieces of dark chocolate instead of a standard chocolate bar could save more than 200 calories?

We aren't here to tell you that any one of these things is a better choice for you, we simply want to draw your attention to these differences, show you what they can mean and empower you to choose for yourself. We'll come back to this and some of the other food-related topics in Chapter 5, but for now, we want to help you understand why we're all about #NoGuilt and why making informed choices about the food you eat is so important.

WT(actual)F(udge)! How is it that the exact same weight of dried banana and fresh banana are almost 500 calories different?!

SWAP THIS	FOR THIS
1 tablespoon mayonnaise (90 calories)	1 tablespoon wholegrain mustard (10 calories)
100 grams dried banana (520 calories)	100 grams fresh banana (89 calories)
1 glass of orange juice (111 calories)	1 whole orange (45 calories)
120 ml of beer (104 calories)	120 ml wine (82 calories)
1 flat white with full cream milk (155 calories)	1 piccolo latte (46 calories)
Tablespoon butter (102 calories)	Tablespoon avocado (24 calories)
Chai latte (200 calories)	Low-calorie hot chocolate (8 calories)
Champagne (100 calories)	Vodka soda (65 calories)
1 large oven-baked potato (265 calories)	1 cup mashed pumpkin (115 calories)
¼ cup sour cream (123 calories)	90 g Greek yoghurt (43 calories)
Can of Coke (161 calories)	Glass of sparkling mineral water with fresh lime (10 calories)
Plain bagel (315 calories)	English muffin (156 calories)
1 cup brown rice (218 calories)	1 cup cauliflower rice (25 calories)
1 cup spaghetti (221 calories)	1 cup zoodles (20 calories)
¼ cup barbecue sauce (104 calories)	¼ cup tomato sauce (54 calories)
¼ cup tomato sauce (54 calories)	1 teaspoon mustard (5 calories)
1 tablespoon olive oil (120 calories)	Spray of olive oil (5 calories)
1 cup full-cream milk (149 calories)	1 cup unsweetened almond milk (30 calories)

The fixed/flexy approach to eating

This technique is one of the cornerstones of this diet, and it's the thing that makes the 3-day diet (almost) impossible to fail at. It's commonly used by naturally slim people to ensure they can enjoy the foods that they want, but not gain any weight. If they have a day that's filled with eating and drinking all the foods they love, they'll balance that out by having a day on either side that is a little more restrained. And if, for whatever reason, they have two relaxed days of eating in a row, they'll rein in their calorie intake for the rest of the week. Most naturally slim people don't even realise that they do this. And if you point this behaviour out to them, they're likely to say something like, 'Well, duh. That's just common sense.'

The problem with many things in life (including this) is that it's only common sense once you know about it. But, too often, people don't take the time to explain things that should be common sense. You need to have that 'aha' moment first. Once you do, you'll think, 'Oh, right. That is common sense.' But until that dawns on you, you're in the dark.

That's why we're breaking that technique down for you here. The ideal way to approach this diet is to balance out each 'off day' with an 'on day' on either side. But if, for whatever reason, you can't do that, all you need to do is reshuffle your 'on day' to make sure you complete three of them each week.

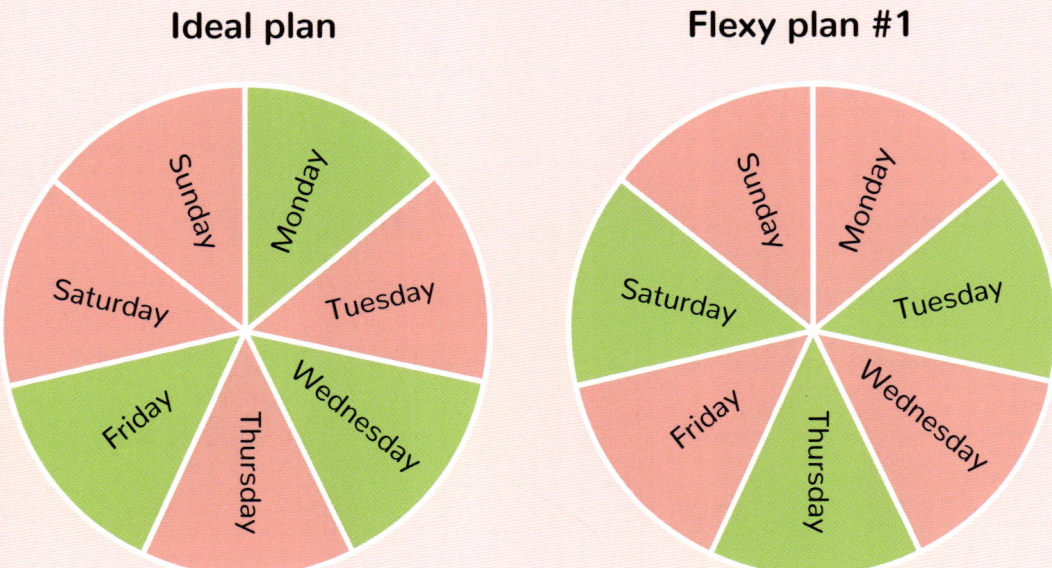

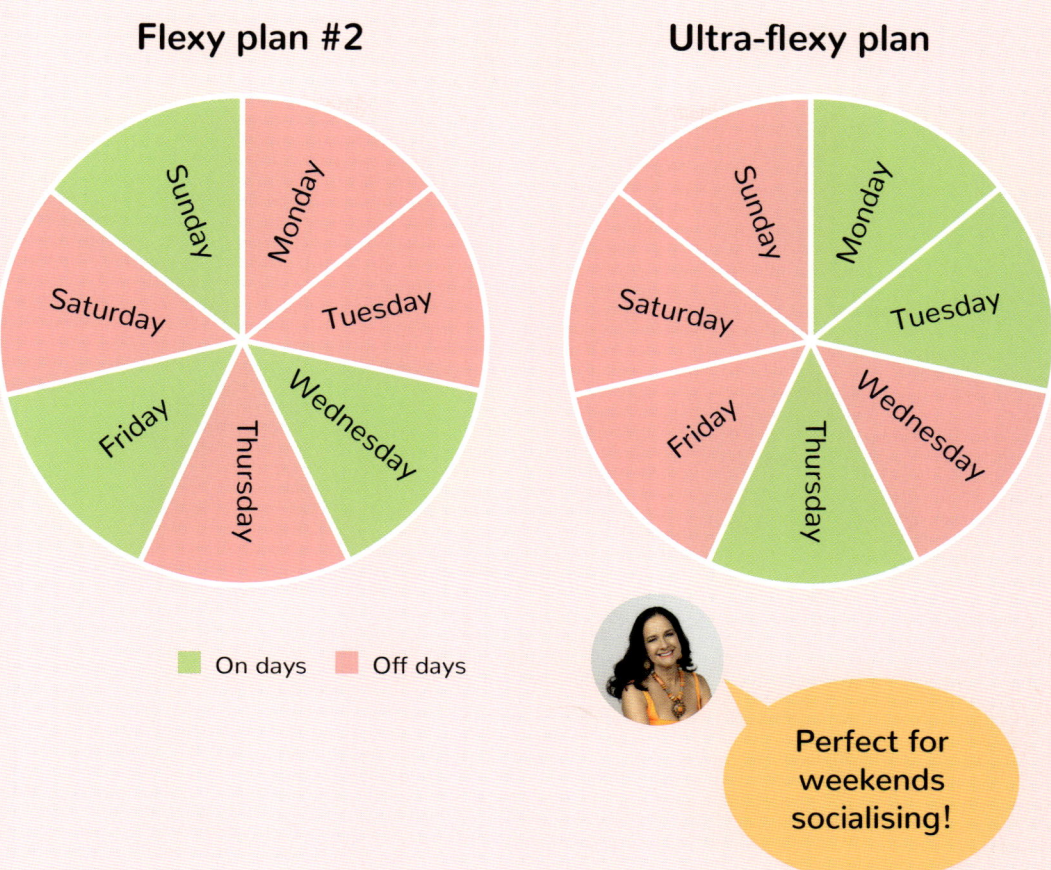

Perfect for weekends socialising!

As you can see, there are some fixed elements to the diet and also some flexible (or flexy) elements. Should you need to take two days off in a row at the beginning of a week or in the middle of a week, you can flex the rest of the week to make sure you fit those three 'on days' in. And with the ultra-flexy plan where you take three days off together (which is far from ideal), you can still fit your 'on days' in by bunching two of them together. For the best results, it's ideal to follow each 'on day' with an 'off day', but life gets busy and sometimes you just might not feel like having an 'on day', which is totally fine! So long as you complete three of them each week, you'll be crushing this 3-day dieting thing.

The major reason traditional diets fail is because they ask people to be 'on' all the time, and that's unsustainable. NO ONE can be good all the time. Trying to be will only make you miserable. We reckon this 3-day diet is as close as it gets to an unbreakable diet. You can flex the heck out of it and take days off. In fact, you can take a few days off, and still come out a winner.

Now you know the basics of 'the answer' you've been searching for, let's step into the future …

CHAPTER 2

Meet the future you

"Impossible is not a *fact*. It's an opinion. Impossible is not a declaration. It's a *dare*."

— Muhammad Ali, boxing legend, activist, entertainer, philanthropist

So you're ready to start

Okay, so we totally get it: now that you know what the 3-day diet is and how easy it is to follow, you're ready to start **NOW**. And you will, but first we want you to think about what succeeding on this diet will look like for 'Future You'.

Every successful person knows that the key to success lies firstly in setting the right goals (in the right way), taking small daily steps towards achieving them, using the best possible tools and techniques, and finally, resting, recharging and rewarding their achievements. So the first thing we're going to tackle is how to set a (realistic) goal weight.

Yay! This is one of the fun bits. And there's a reason this is one of the first things we're tackling: you wouldn't get in the car and expect to end up in the right spot without first deciding on a destination, so how can you expect to start a weight-loss program – or anything for that matter – if you don't know where you want to end up.

There's a mass of research telling us that people who have specific goals and plans are more likely to succeed than those that don't. Goal setting is also a great way – maybe the only way – of measuring your success. After all, how will you know if you're getting there, if you don't know where 'there' is?

American media mogul Ted Turner said, 'You should set goals beyond your reach so you always have something to live for.' And that's a motivating thought when you're in a 'conquer-the-world' mood, but setting goals that are so *big* that they're overwhelming can be more daunting than inspiring. Research shows that setting unrealistic goals is one of the biggest reasons that people become demotivated and eventually give up.

The key is to choose a weight-loss goal that is motivating, achievable and realistic.

Somewhere in the vicinity of 5–10 per cent of your current body weight is generally a good place to start. Most people lose somewhere around 0.5 to 2 kilos per week with our 3-day diet.

Face the scales

Before you can meet 'Future You', first you must completely accept 'Current You', and that is going to mean weighing yourself. Our advice? Do this first thing in the morning after a good, long wee (or, even better, a number two), sans clothes, shoes and anything else that adds weight. Once you know exactly how much you weigh, you can figure out how much you want to lose, and you can begin breaking that larger goal down into smaller mini goals.

It's also useful to measure yourself, as we've found that measurements can occasionally show weight loss before the scales do. We call this the 'WHOOSH' effect, and we LOVE it because it explains why the scales can be so stubborn, even when your pants are a little looser and people are telling you that you look like you've lost weight. See how it works on page opposite.

AFTER

BEFORE

Meet Myles

BEFORE: 122 kg **AFTER:** 93 kg

KILOS GONE 29 kg

With an extremely demanding job in media, Myles absolutely loves going out to lunches and dinners and being social with clients. He also really enjoys having fun with his friends on the weekends, so life revolves around gourmet food and cheeky bevvies.

'What attracted me to the 3-day diet was that I only had to be "good" 3 days a week and I could still wine and dine on the other 4 days, albeit trying to be a little healthier as well. Once I learned how much food you could have on your fast days when you made good choices (like lots of veggies, salads, high-quality proteins), I found it wasn't too hard. Then I could eat, drink and be merry the following day if I wanted. It showed me the types of foods I should be eating and now I actually don't enjoy eating junk food anymore. That's not to say I don't enjoy a treat now and then ... I definitely do, but in moderation. Since dropping around 30 kilos I am so much fitter! I am way more confident and love dressing up to go out. I even found the love of my life ... my beautiful Kate! Kate and I have discovered a passion for cooking nutritious and delicious meals and we go to the gym together most mornings. I never would have done this if I hadn't found this way of life. After years of struggling with my weight, I feel like I've finally nailed it. Life is awesome!'

Intermittent fasting: fat loss – The 'WHOOSH' effect

Why losing weight may take some time

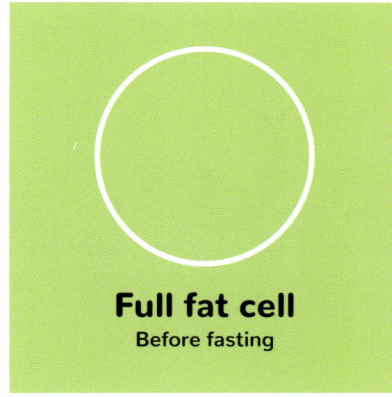

Full fat cell
Before fasting

Fat loss
Cell starts shrinking and waits for fat. You lose weight.

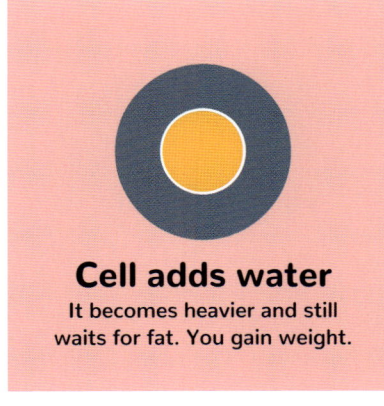

Cell adds water
It becomes heavier and still waits for fat. You gain weight.

Almost no fat
Before collapse, cell is filled with water.

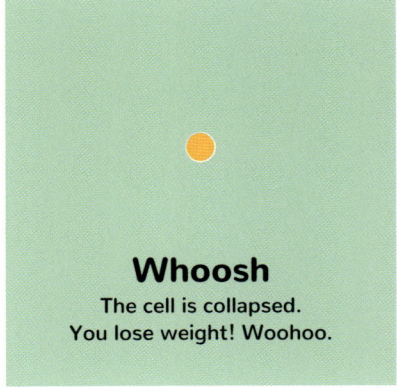

Whoosh
The cell is collapsed.
You lose weight! Woohoo.

Goal setting with the six C's

If you're a fan of big, hairy audacious goals, then, by all means, set one! But do yourself a favour and recognise that it is an ultimate goal. If, for example, losing 10 kilos is your audacious goal, we suggest breaking it into more achievable 2-kilo chunks and rewarding yourself each time you reach one of those mini goals.

Rewarding yourself or reinforcing good behaviour by giving yourself a treat might sound like something that should be reserved for small children and pets, but hear us out. When we treat ourselves, we feel energised – the reward boosts our self-control and our motivation levels. Studies show that people who receive a small treat after accomplishing a goal are far more likely to successfully accomplish their future goals. Author and speaker Gretchen Rubin says, 'If I give more to myself, I can ask more from myself.' Little treats help to combat feelings of deprivation or resentment, which can, in turn, help us to maintain healthy habits for much longer.

Now that you understand a little more about *why* it's important to set a goal weight, it's time to choose one! Eek! We've created an online worksheet to guide you through choosing a healthy goal weight, by taking your height, current weight, lifestyle and daily calorie needs into account.

Go online to superfastdiet.com/3daydietbook to find the worksheet along with other free resources.

The toolkit we're about to share with you, which we call the six C's, has been critical to our own weight-loss success, not to mention the success of many of our SuperFasters. **The six C's are capture, chunk, clear, commit, complete and celebrate.**

Pour yourself a nice cuppa (or a cheeky chardy), sit down and allow yourself a good half hour or so to really focus on your future goal planning. Start with a nice large piece of paper and draw the following pie chart. Next, spend a few minutes visualising yourself as you want to be at the end of your weight-loss journey – really get a detailed mental picture in your head and tune into how good you feel!

Starting with the 'capture' slice of the pie chart, write down a realistic and specific goal, then move clockwise to 'chunk' and detail how you'll break that big goal down into mini-goals. Work your way around the pie until you've revealed your shiny new self. Scribble all over it, write notes, draw pictures, make it yours, and remember to set rewards. They are a huge incentive. Think of them as short-term and long-term presents for yourself. You deserve them!

Now let's bring those goals to life

Now that you've set yourself some bodacious goals, let's pause for a second. Because before you become that person you saw in your mind in the last exercise, we want to help you truly 'see' yourself as that person so we can get your brain on board with what your body is about to do. We're going to do this by using deeper visualisation.

Visualisation gets a bad rap for being a bit 'woo-woo', but research shows that it is a bonafide performance-improvement technique. It works by convincing your brain that you're already doing the thing you wish to be doing. Turns out our neurons (those excitable wires in the brain that transmit information) can't tell the difference between us simply visualising something and actually doing it. So when we turn our full attention to visualising something in our minds, our neurons create a new neural pathway, and this primes our body to act in a way that's consistent with what we've just visualised.

Visualisation can be broken into two techniques: outcome visualisation and process visualisation, and they are best used together for the ideal outcome.

Outcome visualisation is when you visualise yourself as you wish to be in the future – once you've achieved your goal. There are loads of different approaches for this, from journalling to visualisation meditations, but essentially, anything that helps you create a vivid mental picture of yourself achieving a desired goal is suitable. Many of our SuperFasters find that creating a vision board – which can be a physical board or a digital Pinterest board – is helpful when it comes to making their future reality feel more concrete. Ideally, your outcome visualisation should engage as many of your senses as possible because this will convince those neurons that this is already real! To do this, visualise yourself at your goal weight. Think about how amazing you feel, what clothes you're wearing, what you're doing. Ask yourself: What are you eating? What does the air feel like on your skin? What does your goal smell like?

Process visualisation asks you to visualise yourself successfully completing each step of the process towards achieving your goal. This might involve you picturing yourself stepping on the scales, writing down your weight, reading this book, learning how to follow the 3-day diet method, meal prepping on the weekend, then gradually seeing the results each week. It's not quite as fun as outcome visualisation, but it's just as effective, and it can be a handy tool for those who struggle with picturing that end goal.

Visualisation on its own doesn't guarantee success, but it *is* a powerful tool that can improve your performance and improve your chances of success.

Your weight-loss ninja toolkit

Now it's time to get you geared up to smash your goals. You may want to dog-ear this page so you can easily come back to it if you need to. Consider this an easy-to-read roadmap; one that contains everything you need to get to your final destination: Future You.

Helpful apps to download

SuperFastDiet ↓ (of course!) – basically your bible.

Camera or smartphone camera app ↓ for before and after photos! See superfastdiet.com for tips and tricks.

Facebook ↓ to join our 3-day diet group at facebook.com/groups/3daydiet

FitBit, Apple watch or pedometer app ↓ to help you track your daily activity and understand your habits.

YouTube ↓ mainly for cat videos, but there are other cool things on it, too, including our SuperFastDiet videos at youtube.com/superfastdiet

Handy extras

Diary or calendar ↓ for daily planning and goal setting.

Notebook ↓ to help record your successes and thoughts, and to keep lists of rewards you'll gift yourself every time you achieve a goal.

Scales ↓ for throwing in the bin. Jokes! You will need these.

Measuring tape ↓ so you can track every single centimetre you lose.

Pinterest ↓ for creating vision boards and saving recipes.

The 3-Day Diet

CHAPTER 3

Supercharging the 3-day diet

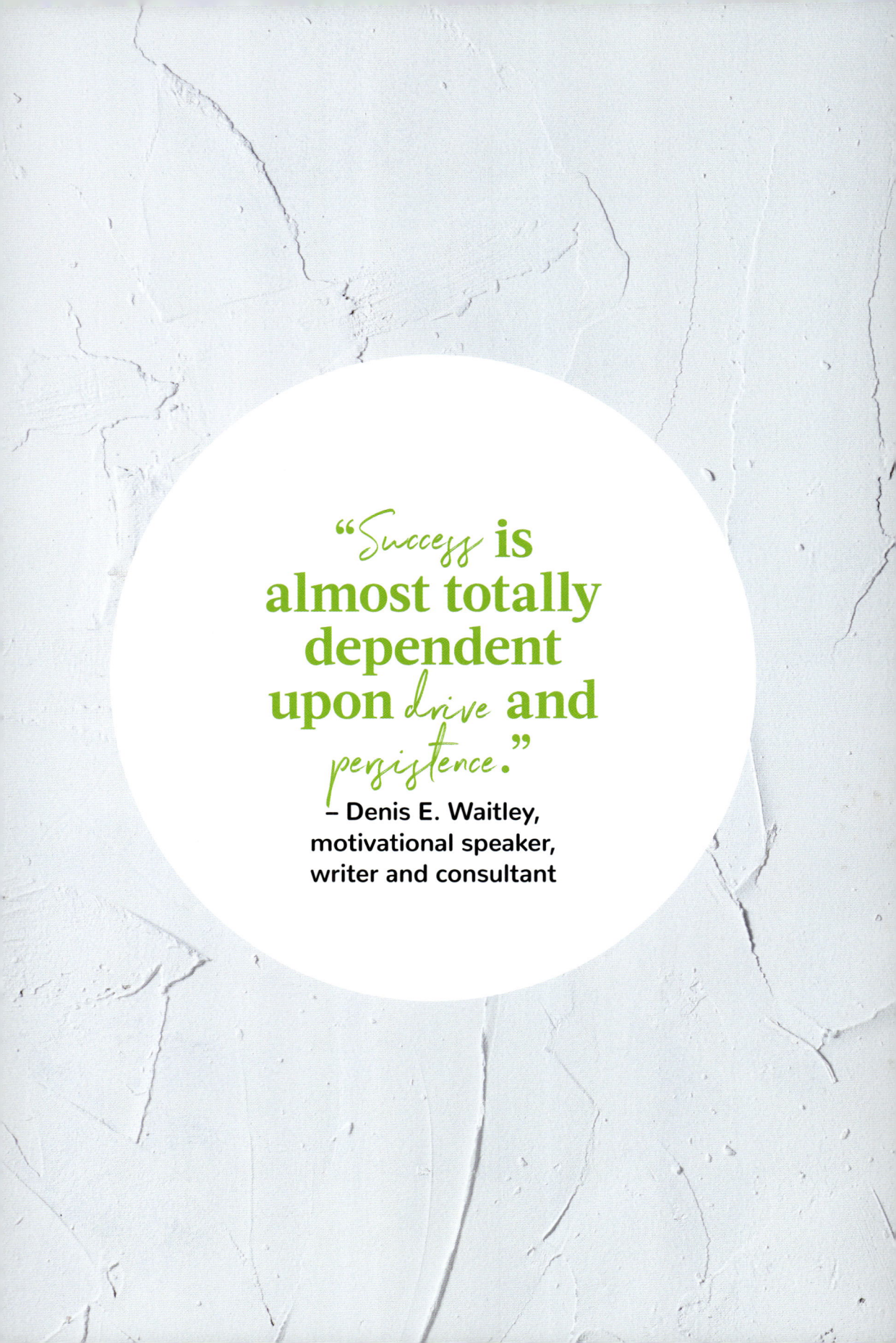

"Success is almost totally dependent upon drive and persistence."

– Denis E. Waitley, motivational speaker, writer and consultant

The supercharging method

First, let's be clear: the 3-day diet will work brilliantly all by itself. But if you want to take your weight loss up a few notches, then combining this method with another one of our methods called 'part-time dieting' might be just the thing. This method is based on an IF method known as 16:8 (because you fast for 16 hours of the day and eat – or 'feast' – within an 8-hour window).

Our circadian rhythms are behind the ebb and flow of our daily lives. They are the rhythms that tell the body and brain when to sleep and when to wake. But you can make them far more powerful than that, and here's how. We typically fast (naturally) for somewhere between eight and twelve hours while we sleep. By extending this period just a skosh, we can stretch out this fasting period to get the maximum possible benefit from it.

When you skip a meal such as breakfast, you start to access your body's fat-burning switch, and when that turns on, your body turns to its own fat stores for fuel (this fat-burning mode is known as 'ketosis'). It's kinda gross, but also kinda cool. We're introducing you to this approach now, because it's such a great way to not only give your body a break from the business of digestion, but also a fab way to make your body's in-built circadian rhythms work for you.

Part of the reason we love 16:8 is because at least eight of those 16 food-free hours are spent sleeping. On top of that, we often don't have time for breakfast anyway, so it feels like we're removing something from that never-ending to-do list rather than adding to it! By the time we've gotten up, had a shower and kick-started our day we only need to distract ourselves for an hour or two and we've burned a whole bunch of extra fat. And then it's time to eat. Win!

Implementing this supercharged approach is as easy as eating within an 8-hour window during the day – and you can do that on your 'on days' and/or your 'off days'. Our favourite eating window is 12 pm to 8 pm because so many of our SuperFasters have had success with this window. (Vic's preferred eating window opens at 1 pm and closes just before 9 pm). It also allows you to still enjoy the social aspects of lunch and dinner, while eliminating the 'to do' aspect of having to prepare breakfast in the mornings.

However, if you're a true breakfast lover and can't face skipping it, you can simply start your eating window earlier in the day. Our members also find the window of 10 am to 6 pm a good one to work with. And if you prefer to eat much earlier, then 8 am to 4 pm is another good option. This supercharging method can be done in the long term, but if you're in maintenance mode then you'll have fewer 'on days' – one or two rather than three.

Wait! Isn't breakfast the most important meal of the day?

According to our mums, yes. But there's pretty much zero scientific evidence for the weight-loss (or metabolic) benefits of eating breakfast. In fact, one of the biggest things we learned when researching and creating the 3-day diet was that it's a-okay to skip breakfast. Forcing down breakfast when we're not hungry is one of the most common ways we sabotage our weight-loss and health goals.

Recent research shows that people who eat breakfast consume an average of 260 calories more each day than those who skip it AND that people who eat breakfast tend to weigh more (by around 0.44 kilos). Basically, skipping breakfast can help to reduce your daily calorie intake, boost your metabolism and give you more time in fat-burning mode.

There have been quite a few studies on skipping breakfast done recently, and of those, most conclude that the benefits of skipping breakfast far outweigh the challenges and disadvantages. Scientists refer to the 16:8 method as 'time-restricted' eating, and here's what they've discovered about people who follow this method:

1. They eat around 20 per cent less, without even trying.

2. They consume somewhere between 200–650 calories less per day than those who eat breakfast.

3. They experience effortless weight loss, improved metabolic fitness and better muscle-mass maintenance.

4. They experience the other benefits typically associated with other IF protocols, such as reductions in 'bad' LDL cholesterol levels and improvements in 'good' HDL cholesterol levels, and reductions in blood sugar and incidence of insulin resistance.

It is true that research done in the 1980s showed that kids did better in school when they ate brekkie first, but those studies didn't measure metabolism or body weight. Recently, scientists agreed that 'most of these studies appear to have been biased in at least one area'. Translation? Breakfast companies most likely sponsored the bulk of the trials that recommended eating breakfast in the first place!

Do I have to count calories if I'm supercharging?

To begin with, yes. We recommend counting calories for maximum results. You still want to stick to **1000** calories on your 'on day' (or whatever half your **TDEE** is). And if you wish to get the maximum benefits of this supercharging approach, we suggest reducing your 'off day' calories by **25** per cent and monitoring what you're eating on those days, too – at least in the beginning, to ensure that you succeed. Since most people can reduce their calorie intake by somewhere between **200** and **650** calories simply by skipping breakfast, this shouldn't be too much of a challenge. Here's how supercharging the 3-day diet looks for an average woman with a **TDEE** of 2000 calories.

3-DAY DIET	SUPERCHARGED VERSION
'ON DAY' = 1000 CALORIES 'OFF DAY' = 2000 CALORIES	'ON DAY' = 1000 CALORIES 'OFF DAY' = 1600 CALORIES

Intermittent fasting purists recommend consuming only zero-calorie beverages like black coffee, tea, water and broth during the fasting window to maximise the amount of time your body spends burning fat, but we've developed some sneaky cheats (more on those on page 51).

If you prefer to keep it super simple (we see you!), just focus on eating within that 8-hour window each day and allow yourself to go up to your full TDEE on your 'off days'.

Go online to find out what a 25 per cent reduction in 'off day' calories looks like for you, head to: superfastdiet.com/3daydietbook

The 3-Day Diet

A typical supercharged 'off day' for an average woman might look like this:

8 am	Wake up, shower, get dressed
9 am	Drink a long black coffee (0 calories)
10 am	Drink a big glass of water or black tea (0 calories)
11 am	Have another glass of water and a cup of bone broth (0 calories)
12 pm (Eating window starts. Yay!)	**BRUNCH OR LUNCH** Enormous chicken salad (320 calories) Plate of fresh fruit (120 calories) Cappuccino (100 calories)
3 pm	**AFTERNOON TEA** Cheese and crackers (212 calories) Cup of tea and milk (45 calories)
6 pm	**SNACK** Bowl of air-popped popcorn (25 calories) Glass of wine (100 calories)
7 pm	**DINNER** Pan-fried fish (150 calories) Salad (50 calories) Roasted potatoes (100 calories) Glass of wine (100 calories)
7.30 pm	**DESSERT** Two pieces of dark chocolate (140 calories)
8 pm	Eating window ends

TOTAL = 1462 calories within the eight hour window (which means there are calories to spare!)

Clean or dirty?
That is the question

When it comes to supercharging the 3-day diet, the question we get asked the most is, 'What can I eat or drink outside the feasting window?' The answer is ... it depends.

If you want to reap the many health benefits of IF and spend longer periods of time in ketosis, then a 'clean' fast is the one for you. 'Clean' means you only consume non-caloric beverages during this period such as water, unflavoured sparkling water, black tea, black coffee or bone broth.

However, we know from experience that this can be too hard for many people (us included!), and especially for those who need to take medication or are trying this method for the first time. So, to help you give it a red-hot go we are big fans of what's known as a 'dirty' fast.

During a dirty fast you can consume up to three beverages under 50 calories each. For example, a skimmed milk or almond milk cappuccino, a cup of tea with a splash of milk, apple cider vinegar in water, kombucha or sparkling water with a hint of fruit or flavouring in it.

Ultimately, the choice is yours. If you're keen to explore this method but you aren't sure you can deal with zero calories for a 16-hour period, start with a dirty fast. Many thousands of our members do this as their lifestyle and get fabulous results.

> Mornings would not be bearable without my trusty almond milk cappuccino. It's dirty ~~dancing~~ fasting all the way for me!

CHAPTER

4

The one where they finally talk about food

"To *eat* is a necessity, but to eat intelligently is an *art*."

– François de La Rochefoucauld,
17th century writer and moralist

This is how we JERF it

You'll be surprised at how much food you can eat when you eat 'intelligently'. At SuperFastDiet HQ, we've mastered the art of getting maximum bang for our calorie buck, and you can, too, by employing some of our tips for low-calorie, high-taste foods.

Learning how to get maximum food for minimum calories is the food equivalent of bargain-hunting for designer clothes! The first (and probably best) tip we're going to give you is also one of the simplest: Just. Eat. Real. Food. #JERF. You'll be surprised at the difference in how you feel and how satisfied you are if you stick to the #JERF ideology for the bulk of your meals.

Real food makes you feel good. It fills you up in ways Frankenfoods can't. There are four essential components to satiety and each of these is monitored by a complex feedback loop between your gut and your brain, which decides if your appetite has been satisfied. When you eat something that doesn't satisfy these four components, you may feel like 'something is missing' after eating. The four essential components of satiety are:

1. **Blood sugar** That feedback loop will monitor whether your blood sugar is rising or falling. Ideally, it will climb slowly and gradually after a meal, rather than quickly and steeply.

2. **Hydration** Consume fresh foods that have a high water content.

3. **Stretch** This describes how (and why) fibre-filled and high-fat content foods will physically 'fill' your belly. This is often part of the reason Frankenfoods, sugary treats and refined carbohydrates leave us feeling hungry and dissatisfied, even with their high calorie content.

4. **Nutrient content** Your body monitors its vitamin and mineral levels, and will trigger specific cravings in order to hunt down foods that fulfil specific vitamin and mineral requirements. It's often why we crave salty foods after eating a lot of sugar; that's our body's way of telling us to eat something that will satisfy our vitamin and mineral requirements. And this is often why people mistake thirst or vitamin deficiencies for hunger.

So, yes, calorie content is important. But so is water content, fibre content, fat content and nutrient content. By prioritising foods that contain all four of these elements, you'll be able to build meals (and snacks) that make you feel full and satisfied. And that's a win–win.

You can eat it all (Yes, really)

Counting macros is all the rage, but we don't subscribe to this approach because it's a bit on the 'gym junkie' side of things for us. Why overthink something that's already been overthought to the extreme? Food doesn't need to be so complicated. A little common sense and a few basic guidelines go a long way.

When it comes to food, we prefer to do as the late aeronautical engineer Kelly Johnson suggested and KISS: keep it simple, sweetheart. Eat a little bit of everything. Taste the macronutrient rainbow. To be healthy humans, we need to enjoy a balanced, moderate intake of everything.

The 1, 2, 3, 4 approach

Happily, there is a super-simple way to guide your portions and ensure you're getting the right balance of macronutrients without overthinking things, reaching for the calculator every time you get hungry or using seven different apps. We call it the 1, 2, 3, 4 approach, because it's a very simple four-step approach that essentially makes balancing every meal as easy as child's play.

Remember back in Chapter 1 when we showed you how to split your 1000 calorie allowance on an 'on day'? Well, here's a very simple way to remember those recommendations:

100 CALORIES FOR SNACKS

200 CALORIES FOR BREAKFAST

300 CALORIES FOR LUNCH

400 CALORIES FOR DINNER

And we've got *another* easy component to this approach that will allow you to effortlessly put together perfectly balanced meals, without calorie counting or weighing food.

The easy-peasy, no calorie-counting approach (aka success in the palm of your hand)

If you're keen to incorporate the 3-day diet without having to think too hard about counting calories or weighing food, you can use the 1, 2, 3, 4 handful approach to manage your portions. Generally speaking, 100 calories of the right type of foods (think nuts, berries, veggies, lean protein) tends to equal about a handful. Two hundred calories is around two handfuls, 300 calories is about three handfuls ... you see where we're going with this.

You can use this approach to build your meals without needing to count calories or weigh food. You can use your hand to estimate the protein servings below:

- the palm to estimate red meat servings
- the size of your hand out flat to estimate white meat and fish servings
- the end of your thumb to estimate oil, sauce and butter serving sizes.

Main meals (lunch and dinner) can comprise approximately:

1 palmful of protein

2 handfuls of veggies

3 no more than ⅓ of your plate of clever carbohydrates (see box below)

4 teaspoons maximum for fat, butter and oils

What the heck are clever carbs?

Clever carbs are the smarter, more talented siblings of the refined carbohydrate. Modern refined carbs – pasta, white rice, bread – are simple carbohydrates that have been processed to remove all the good bits such as fibre, vitamins and nutrients. Clever carbs, on the other hand, are more than just carbohydrates because they are way more nutritious and can help you reach your goals by giving you MORE energy, MORE satisfaction and maximum bang for your calorie buck. They incorporate everything from starchy and root vegetables, such as pumpkin, sweet potato, carrots, peas and corn, to wholegrains, such as oats, bran and dark rye, linseed and soy, legumes, such as beans, lentils and split peas, and wholegrain pasta and noodles, along with brown rice like basmati or Doongara. When you incorporate carbs into your diet, make them clever carbs and you'll notice a big difference in how you feel, how much energy you have and how much weight you lose.

Note The 1, 2, 3, 4 approach shouldn't be used to estimate refined carbohydrate calories or the calorie content of sugary snacks, as they tend to vary wildly in size and calorie content. However, as these shouldn't be too much of your 'on day' food content anyway, if you're eating for maximum satiety and minimal calories, this won't be an issue.

The 3-Day Diet

How to grocery shop like a pro

Grocery shopping can be a thankless, stressful task, but thankfully we've developed some sneaky tips over the past few years to make it simpler and a lot less painful. These are our three golden rules for grocery shopping.

1 **Stick to the perimeter of the store:** That's where you'll find the good stuff: vegetables, fruit, dairy, meat, fish and health foods.

2 **If you do need items from the centre aisles, dip in and get out quick:** The centre aisles tend to contain Frankenfoods and unnecessary items. Wandering up and down these aisles will only distract you from your list and ensure you end up with things in your trolley that you just don't need.

3 **Implement a rule of thirds in your shopping trolley:** By breaking your trolley into thirds, and filling each third according to this golden rule, you'll be getting a great balance of the good stuff. Here's how it works in an ideal world:

1/3 fresh fruit, vegetables and clever carbs	1/3 meat, dairy and proteins	1/3 treats like coffee and maybe some dark chocolate
- Leafy greens - Cruciferous veggies (kale, broccoli, bok choy) - Beans and pulses - Root vegetables - Onions, leek, garlic - Apples and pears - Berries - Stone fruits - Citrus fruit - Tropical fruit - Wholegrain wraps - Wholegrain or sourdough bread	- Fish - Eggs - Red meat - Plant-based proteins - Low-calorie and low-salt deli meats - Tofu - Nuts - Dairy - Cheese - Yoghurt	- Coffee and tea - Popcorn - Dark chocolate - Low-calorie items (konjac noodles, etc.) - Diet drinks and soups - Seaweed, crackers - Olive oil and pickles - Antipasti (e.g. sun-dried tomatoes and olives)

Low-cal legends

We know from experience that it's crucial to have some low-calorie staples on hand for those 'on days'. They will always get you out of trouble if you find yourself wavering. Here are some of our go-tos.

ALMOST NO CALORIES	25–30 CALORIES	35–40 CALORIES	50–60 CALORIES
• Celery sticks • Lettuce • Pickles • Cucumbers • Green capsicums • Mushrooms • Cauliflower • Zucchini • Broccoli	• 1 small mandarin • ½ cup of watermelon • ¼ rockmelon • 1 small tomato • 1 carrot • 1 cup popcorn • 12 thin pretzel sticks • 100 grams pumpkin	• 1 peach • 1 nectarine • ½ grapefruit • ½ cup skim milk • ¼ cup plain yoghurt • 2 saltine crackers • ½ banana	• 1 small apple • 1 small orange • 15 grapes • 12 cherries • 1 cup strawberries • ¼ cup cottage cheese • 4 small prawns

Hmm, I can't help but notice that there's no column on page 60 for 'fun stuff'.

Don't stress, Victoria. This is just for your three 'on days'. You can have all the vitamin W(ine) and C(heesy Doritos) you like on your four 'off days'.

Hacks for busy peeps

There are a few handy modern tools and tricks that will enable you become a meal-prep ninja and help you stick to your fast day calorie allowance. Items such as these can help you prep for the week on a Sunday afternoon, then not have to think about the food you're eating for the rest of the week.

Useful gadgets and gizmos

- **Kitchen scales:** to guide portions and weigh food.
- **Grater:** for grating cauliflower, zucchini and oodles of cheese for your Friday-night pizza.
- **Blender or food processor:** it makes mash, pizza bases and cauliflower rice much faster (but also for Friday-night cocktails, because your cheesy pizza deserves a friend).
- **Water bottle or jug:** to remind you to hydrate and for mixing iced and fruit teas.
- **And, in the 'nice to have' category:** spiraliser or zoodle maker, mandolin, popcorn maker, air-fryer, waffle maker … Whatever floats your boat in the gadget department.
- **Bento boxes:** for snacks.
- **BPA-free plastic containers:** we like JuggleBox for storing food.
- **Ziplock bags:** for portioning out nuts and popcorn (reuse these for minimal environmental impact).
- **Aluminium foil or baking paper:** for baking protein like chicken and fish, and for wrapping lunchtime wraps.
- **Glassware:** for pre-prepared soups and veggies.
- **Jars:** for pre-prepped 'shake and serve' salads (or funky hipster cocktails).
- **Water infuser:** for fruit teas.

Prepping timesavers

Save stacks of time during the week by doing these things at the weekend. You'll thank us, we promise.

- Pre-boiling and peeling eggs.
- Baking and shredding protein like chicken breast.
- Washing, de-seeding and chopping veggies like cucumber, lettuce and capsicum for salads.
- Pre-rinsing and cooking grains like quinoa or brown rice.
- Pre-roasting your favourite root vegetables for healthy breakfasts and lunch bowls.

Grab-and-go fixes for busy peeps

Here are a few more goodies to add to your shopping lists for those 'on days'. We call them our 'handbag handies'. They've saved us many times, so don't leave home without them!

- Tin of tuna in springwater 95 g (90 calories)
- Low-calorie soup (50 calories)
- Boiled egg (78 calories) Just FYI, we don't recommend leaving this in your handbag or glove box!
- Bag of air-popped popcorn (30 calories)
- Punnet of blackberries (80 calories)
- Punnet of baby tomatoes (45 calories)
- Handful of almonds (about 14) or pistachios (100 calories)
- Bone broths and powdered stocks (0 calories)
- Green tea and fruit tea (0 calories)
- Small piece of fruit (60–80 calories)
- Beef jerky (90–100 calories)
- Seaweed and nori snacks (70 calories)
- 10 rice crackers (70 calories)
- 100 g edamame (120 calories)

Our 'on days' on a plate

Fast days don't have to be boring! All it takes is a little planning and you can have a very satisfying, yummy day. Here are our easy-peasy no-recipe days . . .

Victoria's fast day

BREAKFAST	Skinny cappuccino (90 calories) 12 strawberries (70 calories) 2 tablespoons Greek yoghurt (40 calories)
LUNCH	Pumpkin soup (130 calories) Sandwich thin (toasted, to dip into soup) (117 calories)
SNACKS	Small mandarin (40 calories) 1 plum (30 calories) Handful almonds (70 calories)
DINNER	100 g pan-fried ocean perch (117 calories) 2 cups steamed veggies (100 calories) 1 cup baked pumpkin (30 calories)
DESSERT	1 square dark chocolate (56 calories) Low-calorie drinking chocolate (50 calories)

TOTAL = 940 calories

Gen's fast day

BREAKFAST	Black coffee (0 calories) Boiled egg (78 calories) 2 Corn thins or rice cakes with 2 cheese slices (10 g total) and sliced tomato (120 calories)
LUNCH	1 serve konjac noodles (10 calories) with mushrooms, tomato, celery (about 50 calories) cooked in ½ tin of tomatoes (50 calories)
SNACKS	1 cup rockmelon, grapes or cherries (50 calories) Handful pistachios (100 calories)
DINNER	100 g grilled chicken (165 calories) 2 cups salad (50 calories) 20 g feta (50 calories)
DESSERT	1 cup Greek yoghurt (170 calories) with a drizzle of manuka honey (50 calories) Cup of chamomile tea (0 calories)

TOTAL = 943 calories

Go online to see more of our 'on days' on a plate: superfastdiet.com/what-do-you-eat-on-a-fast-day

The one where they finally talk about food

CHAPTER

5

Enjoy the things that make life worth living

"I'd much rather eat *pasta* and drink *wine* than be a size zero."

– Sophia Loren, actress

Eat, drink and be merry ... for tomorrow we fast!

Believe it or not, you CAN indulge, go out and socialise without going overboard. Once you get into the rhythm of the 3-day diet, you'll begin to get more comfortable and realise that you don't have to make up for being on a diet by going completely crazy when you do go out. The beauty of this approach is having those days off every week, so you don't feel like you need to make up for anything. And, because no food is forbidden, the allure of breaking your diet or saying, 'To hell with it' and throwing the whole thing out the window, doesn't really exist.

The question is: how do you indulge without going overboard? Well, in the years we've been designing this diet, we've come up with a few sneaky tips and tricks to do just this. You'll be surprised at the difference that some very small tweaks can make. Below are some of our best tips and tricks.

- Eat any veggies on offer first when you are out – they'll fill you up and make you less susceptible to reaching for things like bread rolls and fries.
- Space out alcoholic drinks by drinking glasses of water between them. You'll consume fewer calories and keep yourself hydrated (not to mention more sober).
- Split a dish with a friend. Most restaurant dishes are ridiculously oversized, so this will save you calories and cash!
- Always order sauces on the side and dip into them rather than pouring them all over your meal. You'll find you'll use a lot less.
- Use your thumb to measure out portions of butter and sauce rather than guesstimating.
- Swap fruity and creamy cocktails for lighter options like a vodka soda or dry champagne and you'll save stacks of calories.

Every weekend I say to myself, 'Jane, you have to stop drinking wine.' (Thankfully, I'm not Jane.)

Sugar is a she-devil

Oh sweet, delicious sugar. We love you so, but you're oh-so-bad for us. You've heard the saying that sugar is as addictive as heroin, right? Well, turns out that's not far from the truth. Countless studies have looked at the effects that sugar has on our body, and scientists have realised that sugar is not only insanely addictive, it also messes with our body and neurochemistry in a boatload of ways.

One of the not-so-great effects of sugar has to do with a hormone called ghrelin, which is produced in the gut. Ghrelin makes us feel hungry when we need fuel. The hormone leptin has the opposite effect: it tells the brain and body when we're satisfied or full. Well, too much sugar can cause the brain to stop recognising leptin. In fact, sugar can make your body and brain resistant to leptin. Imagine not being able to ever feel satisfied or full! This is commonly known as leptin resistance, and it's one of the reasons why the two of us like to call sugar a basic b**ch! It's also one of the reasons people who consume a lot of sugar always seem to be hungry and often feel dissatisfied or grumpy, no matter how much they eat.

So, not only does sugar add a stack of calories to your diet and make you hungrier, it also contributes to a metric tonne of other health issues including acne, cardiovascular disease, metabolic syndrome, diabetes and cancer.

How can you tell if you're addicted to sugar?

- [ ] You need increasing amounts to satisfy your cravings.
- [ ] You eat sugar even when you're not hungry and you always crave sweets.
- [ ] You may have even begun to hide your sugar habit. (Sorry, secret stash of Tim Tams, you've got to go.)
- [ ] You consume sweets to soothe yourself or cope with stress or boredom.
- [ ] You go out of your way to get it (a surefire sign of addiction).
- [ ] You crave salty foods (a biological sign that you're not getting enough nutrition).
- [ ] You've tried to quit in the past and have experienced withdrawal symptoms.

Despite the sugary doom and gloom it *is* okay to have a sweet tooth! Enjoying treats like lollies, cake, chocolate or even brownies doused in Baileys (thanks for that one, Victoria) is *totally* human. In fact, it's one of the best things in life. But sometimes a sweet tooth tips over from being a little indulgence to an insatiable issue. And when you consume too much sugar for too long, your brain essentially rewires itself to crave sugar – so much so that many people even experience withdrawal symptoms when they try to give it up or make the switch to a healthier lifestyle.

Some of these withdrawal symptoms include headaches, uncontrollable lethargy or fatigue, craving salty foods, muscle pain, nausea, bloating and insomnia. These kinds of symptoms generally show up at around the 24-hour mark and tend to intensify over the following days, which is why many people find it so difficult to give up sugar. The best way to completely kick the habit without these painful withdrawal symptoms is to cut back little by little.

The maximum recommended sugar intake is 6 teaspoons (or 24 grams) per day. But many Westerners consume a whopping 40 teaspoons (160 grams). We're not going to tell you to stop eating sugar, but we will say that you'll feel so much better if you eat just a little bit less of it.

Sugar substitutes that don't suck

Although it's ideal to set yourself a goal of no more than the maximum recommended sugar intake, sometimes the best way to start reducing your reliance on sugar is to try replacing it with something else. There are many sugar substitutes on the market and almost all of them are man-made. Controversy abounds about how healthy (or downright dangerous) they may be. There are, however, four sugar substitutes that we do think are worth considering:

1. **Stevia:** At 0 calories, this is our favourite option as it's naturally derived from the leaf of the stevia plant.

2. **Monk fruit:** Another calorie-free naturally derived option that comes from monk fruit juice (as you would expect). It can be a little hard to find but health-food shops should stock it if your local supermarket doesn't.

3. **Aspartame:** Comes in at 4 calories per gram and is sold under the brand names NutraSweet and Equal.

4. **Saccharin:** 0 calories, this is often combined with aspartame in soft drinks.

10 tasty AF snacks that really should be illegal

Do you have cravings that you just can't seem to satisfy with 'diet-friendly food'? Don't stress. Been there, done that, bought the overpriced T-shirt. Feast your eyes on our favourite snack hacks to satisfy a sweet tooth or salty craving without derailing your good work.

1 cup popcorn
(27 calories)

130 g kale chips
(108 calories)

1 glass kombucha or sugar-free soft drink
(8 calories)

10 fresh raspberries
(10 calories)

Enjoy the things that make life worth living

½ cup frozen pineapple

(40 calories)

60 raisins

(90 calories)

3 chocolate dipped strawberries

(60 calories)

2 squares of dark chocolate

(112 calories)

40 g edamame

(44 calories)

¼ cup hummus with a few crackers

(194 calories)

The 3-Day Diet

Beware the restaurant dessert!

Not only do restaurants *not* tend to adhere to normal serving sizes, they also tend to serve their desserts with a bunch of side ingredients such as whipped cream, biscuits, sorbet or ice cream. This makes it difficult to properly estimate the calorie content of what you order (especially if you've had a few wines or cocktails first). Take a look at the wildly varying calorie counts in the brownies on this page.

Granted, many of us probably wouldn't be able to finish off a restaurant dessert like this. But we may well get two-thirds of the way through it. And even that is a whopping 600-odd calories, which could very quickly throw your 'off day' from a very reasonable 2000 calories to nearly 3000 calories. And since, generally speaking, most of us only need to consume an additional 7000 calories or so to gain 1 kilo, you can see how little things like this can make a massive difference to your success.

TOTAL CALORIES = 905.5

Home-made brownie or supermarket version

ONE BROWNIE
serving size 24 grams
(112 calories)

TOTAL CALORIES = 112

Restaurant version

NUTELLA BROWNIE
serving size 48 grams
(224 calories)

+

two scoops vanilla ice cream
(274 calories)

+

brown sugar nut crumble on top
(212 calories)

+

a spoonful of Nutella on top
(80 calories)

+

caramel drizzle on plate
(115.5 calories)

TOTAL CALORIES = 905.5

Is it wine o'clock?

Wine is quite calorific, so overindulging can really sabotage your efforts. For example, if you enjoy around three to four restaurant-sized glasses over the course of a meal (which falls somewhere between six and eight standard servings), then the calorie count of your wine is somewhere between 720 calories and 1000 calories, depending on your wine of choice. Surprisingly high, huh?

That's not to say you must forego wine completely; you can simply be smart about how you choose to consume it. By measuring your glass, you'll be aware of how much you're consuming. And by choosing varieties that are lower in sugar, you'll be able to enjoy a few glasses without sabotaging your success on the scales.

Health authorities recommend no more than 1.4 drinks a day and no more than four drinks on any one occasion. Your 'on days' are ideal days to make alcohol-free choices. And this is a great habit your body will thank you for.

Wine or dessert? Choose one, save a tonne

A little trick we've used over the years is to make a choice between wine and dessert when having a fancy dinner out. We choose one, never both. By deciding between them you can help to make sure that you don't undo all your progress on those nights out.

Dynamite drops that won't sabotage your success

Even though you don't have to give up wine in order to lose weight, it's worth educating yourself about some of the lower-calorie drops available. You'll be surprised at the difference they can make! There are a few savvy ways to ensure you choose a drop with a lot less calories than your average vino.

Generally, dry wines are the best bet as they contain less sugar overall than sweeter varieties. Similarly, lighter reds will be less calorific than their fuller-bodied counterparts. On the whole, white wine tends to contain slightly fewer calories than red.

Very best low-cal white wine choices
- Zero-dosage Champagne (see note)
- Champagne extra-brut (this is extra-dry and overlaps with zero-dosage)
- Any dry sparkling wine

Honorable mentions
- Pinot grigio
- A dry riesling
- Sauvignon blanc
- A dry gewurztraminer

Very best low-cal red wine choices
- Pinot noir
- Cabernet sauvignon
- Merlot

What does 'zero-dose' mean?

Traditionally, when champagne is bottled, a tiny amount of sweet wine and maybe even Cognac (or '*dosage*') is added to the bottle. The sweetness of the dosage balances out the dry acidity of the sparkling wine. Wines and champagnes that don't have this added are drier than most, and known as 'zero-dose', 'dosage zèro, 'pas dose', 'Brut nature' or 'sauvage'. Or even 'sugar free'.

Tip Steer clear of port, sweet sherry and late-harvest varieties of wine. These are commonly much higher in sugar and thus calories.

The 3-Day Diet

Super skinny drinks for savvy socialisers

Being the social butterflies we are, we've discovered a few other super-skinny drinks that'll allow you to enjoy a tipple without too many calories. Say 'cheers to clears' and opt for wine, champagne, beer and hard spirits served over ice, rather than fruity or creamy cocktails.

Avoid mixers, juices and tonic water wherever you can, and opt for fresh flavours over bottled cordials. This may mean asking the bartender if the flavours in your drink come from real fruit or from syrups, and requesting adjustments like a splash of this, a drop of that or a half serving of something.

Here are a few of our favourite tipples.

Vodka, fresh lime and soda

65 calories

Mojito (hold the syrup)

100 calories

Frosé (that's frozen rosé. Delish!)

150 calories

Champagne cocktail

135 calories

Tequila and fresh lime

180 calories

Gin and diet tonic

120 calories

We have one more tipple tip to share before we leave the good times behind! If you don't feel like imbibing, but still want to feel like you're treating yourself, try some new alcohol-free drinks instead. There are many options these days from distilled spirits (think Seedlip) that mimic gin, rum and even Aperol, to low (or no) alcohol wines and beer. Check out sansdrink.com.au for sassy sober inspo.

And let's not forget the humble sparkling mineral water with a squeeze of fresh lemon or lime. Zero cals and maximum feel-good factor.

Vodka and kombucha
90 calories

Bloody Mary
105 calories

Martini (sans vermouth)
128 calories

Light beer
104 calories

Hot toddy (whisky and hot water)
150 calories

> How good is saying 'bottoms up' while the size of your actual bottom is going down. (Cheeky!)

CHAPTER

6

Mindset 101: strategies to supersize your success

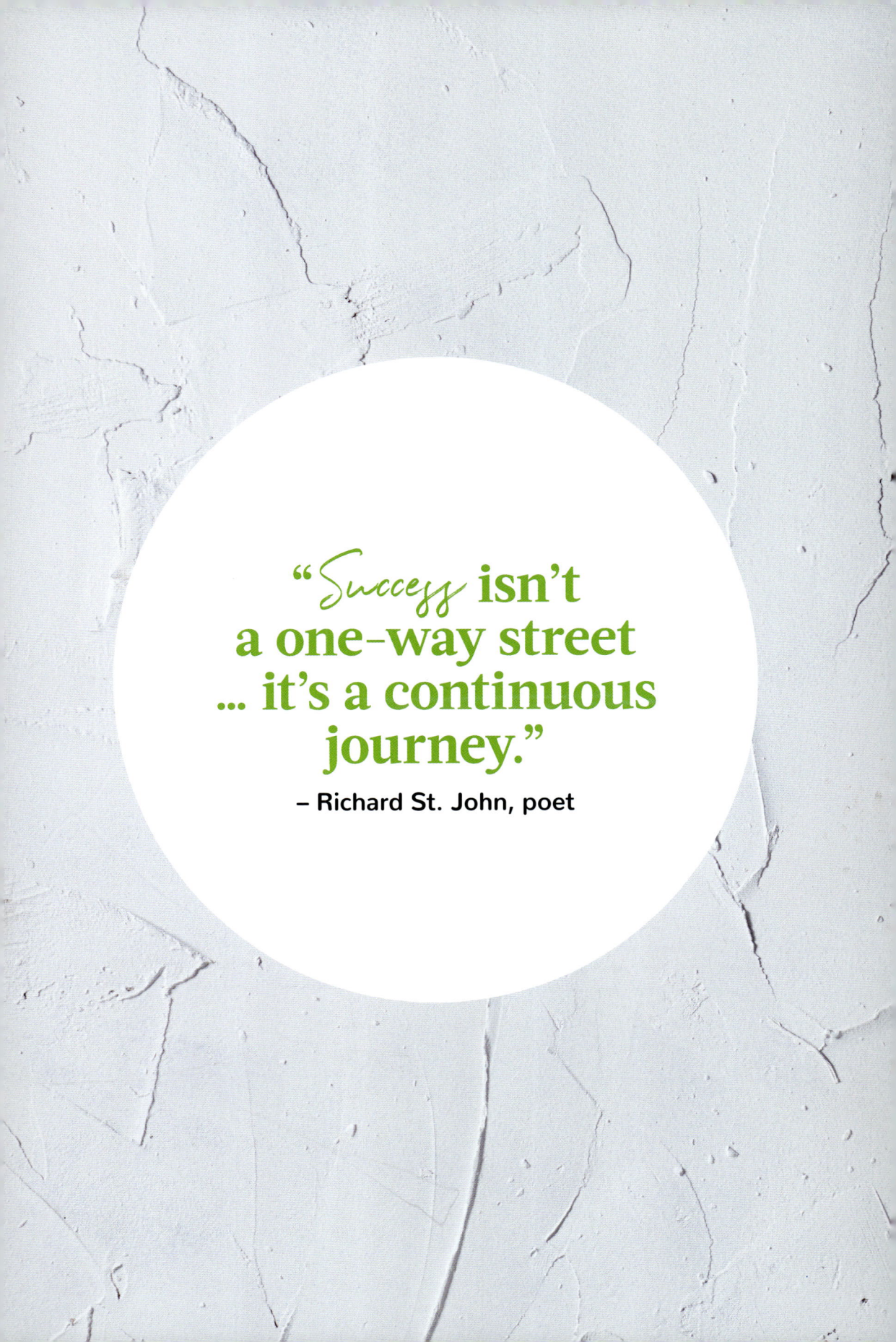

"*Success* isn't a one-way street ... it's a continuous journey."

– Richard St. John, poet

The six habits of successful slimmers

Mindset matters, but not in the way that most people think. A lot of self-proclaimed weight-loss and fitness gurus use the term 'mindset' in the context of forcing yourself to do something that you don't feel like doing. But when we say that mindset matters, we mean being kind to yourself matters. Becoming your own biggest cheerleader matters. Learning to become your own best friend matters. Those 'go hard or go home', 'just do it', 'beastmode ... RAHHH!' mentalities only really work when you're feeling good. When you're down, tired, stressed or anxious, they'll only make you feel like crap. And that's not why we're here.

We're here to make you feel good, dammit. That's why we've identified the elements of mindset that we think truly matter; these are also the approaches that have helped our SuperFastDiet community of tens of thousands of people successfully reach their goal weight and make this their way of life.

Mindset (or 'lifeset' is probably a more accurate term) is such a big thing to us that we've dedicated an entire third pillar of our online program to it. Our three pillars are: SuperFast, SuperFood and SuperLife. And SuperLife is made up of six habits that, when strengthened over time, come together to create one big, fabulous SuperLife: movement, mindset, happiness, rest, giving and style.

The reason we include this SuperLife pillar in our approach is because success is very one-sided without it. Western culture's current definition of success involves having money and power, but as Arianna Huffington points out in her book *Thrive*, this is not sustainable; it's 'like a two-legged stool – you can balance on it for a while, but eventually you're going to topple over. And more and more people – very successful people – are toppling over.'

There's no point being slim and physically healthy if you're woefully unhappy or lonely or never at peace. Or if your mind is so full of worry that you can't enjoy life. What tends to happen when we succeed without incorporating this third pillar is that we enjoy success, but only in that fleeting moment. After we achieve our goal and get wherever it is we were going, we realise that Gertrude Stein was right: 'There is no *there* there.' This is why the six habits that make up our SuperLife pillar are such a critical part of our approach.

Habit 1: Mastering positive self-talk (aka positive mindset)

One of the elements of our program that resonates the most with our SuperFasters is the concept of the mean girl (or guy). Most of us have a meanie inside our head that chatters away incessantly. In fact, it's so common that Melissa Abrosini wrote a bestseller all about it called *Mastering Your Mean Girl*. More often than not, our inner meanie says critical things like, 'Oh wow, that was a dumb thing to do!' or 'You're a moron' or 'You sounded really stupid when you said that.' That isn't the only form of negative thinking we can be guilty of though. Here are four more really common ones:

1. **Magnifying:** Focusing only on the negative aspects of a situation and ignoring the positives.

2. **Catastrophising:** Expecting the worst and not letting reason or logic persuade you to think otherwise.

3. **Polarising:** Seeing the world only as good or bad, black or white. Failing to recognise that there are, more often than not, shades of grey and a middle ground.

4. **Personalising:** Blaming yourself for everything.

Full disclosure: both of us have had to battle with negative thinking and our mean girls for a big portion of our lives – so we get how hard it can be to shut her down. But we promise that your life will become unimaginably better if you can turn your inner mean girl into your inner cheerleader.

Here's the thing: no one hears what you say to yourself inside your own head, except you. So why not turn that inner chatter into something that's going to serve you more effectively. Why not make that negative self-talk *positive*? Or at the very least, learn how to tell your mean girl to 'bugger the heck off'. She's not you. She's part of you, but she's not the whole you. You are so much more complex and amazing and unique and shiny and sparkly than just that one voice.

Your inner dialogue has the capacity to not only change what's going on in your head, but to have huge health benefits, too. The science shows that people who master positive self-talk and an optimistic outlook display the following:

- 35 per cent lower chance of heart disease
- 14 per cent lower chance of early death
- Lower blood sugar and cholesterol
- Reduced chances of infection
- Reduced chances of cancer
- 15 per cent longer life expectancy
- 50 per cent greater chance of living past the age of 85
- Reduced pain
- Greater immune function
- Better physical wellbeing.

Become your own BFF

One of the ways you can begin becoming your own BFF is to be more mindful of the inner dialogue that you're replaying over and over again. Just because you *think* something doesn't make it true. Let's hear that again: Just because you think something doesn't make it true. Practise catching those negative thoughts and reframing them as positives. For example: 'I've failed and I'm embarrassed,' might become: 'I'm proud of myself for trying! That took courage.' And 'I'm so overweight and out of shape' could become: 'I'm strong and capable and I deserve to feel healthier!' The more you can reframe thoughts in this way, the faster you'll succeed in many areas of life, and the healthier and happier you'll become. Go to superfast.com/3daydietbook to find the online worksheet to get you started on that path.

Habit 2: Exercise – the ultimate mood booster

One of the main reasons people struggle with exercise is because they do it to lose weight, rather than to enjoy it in and of itself. If you approach movement as something that will benefit your mind rather than your body, you'll find it so much easier to stick to. There are so many studies showing that exercise decreases stress and reduces symptoms of anxiety by pumping up endorphin levels and improving our mood, while simultaneously creating vibrant new brain cells and shutting down those that shouldn't be in action. In fact, one review concluded that a whopping 91 per cent of all surveys showed that exercise provided effective results in controlling and reducing symptoms of depression.

> Do it for your brain, and your booty!

Habit 3: Happiness – hop off the hedonic treadmill

There's a theory related to human behaviour called the *hedonic treadmill* or *hedonic adaptation*. Basically, it means that it's human nature to be always chasing the next thing. We may experience a brief period of happiness after we achieve that 'thing', but then there's something else we want. Whether that's another weekend away, a new pair of shoes, a new house or to lose weight, we're always chasing something.

Happiness isn't situation dependent. We often think it is, but in reality, the happiest people in the world are able to be happy under any circumstances. And getting happy actually helps you to lose weight more easily because, quite simply, everything is a lot easier when you're already happy. So, rather than deciding that you'll be happy *when X happens*, decide to be happy now. Want more incentive? Here's how being happy can help you lose weight.

- People who are unhappy and stressed tend to have higher cortisol levels, which is a hormone that can increase cravings, which can in turn cause an even lower mood. And stress makes your body hold on to fat for dear life!
- You'll be more able to find pleasure in things other than food.
- You'll make better decisions.
- You'll eat better.
- You'll get more sleep.
- You won't be as hard on yourself when you do stumble.
- You'll be more resilient.

Habit 4: Rest – don't snooze? You lose!

Resting and relaxing aren't just great excuses to switch off and lounge around, they are fundamental to our survival and our ability to live our best lives. Taking time out to rest, recharge and relax is not only a habit of highly successful slimmers, it's also a habit of highly successful people. Why? Because the mind and body need regular breaks to stay in tip-top condition.

When we sleep, we suspend our consciousness and our body shuts off most of its major functions. Aside from breathing, cardiovascular function and deeper mental tasks like memory consolidation, the body and mind are essentially in 'off' mode. Our muscles repair, our digestion takes a break, our brain sorts through information and experiences, our immune system releases anti-inflammatory proteins to fight infection, and our pituitary gland releases growth hormone to help our body grow and repair itself.

Did you know that your brain basically washes itself while you sleep? In 2015, researchers discovered that our synapses (the connections between neurons that allow them to communicate with one another) shrink by around 20 per cent while we sleep. Another study, in 2019, discovered that cerebrospinal fluid (the clear fluid that cushions your brain and fills your spinal cord) floods into the brain during non-REM sleep, flushing out waste products and toxic proteins, such as amyloid plaques, which have been associated with neurodegenerative diseases, such as Alzheimer's. Understanding these night-time happenings explains why you might feel slow or struggle to think clearly when you haven't had your full forty winks.

How much sleep do we need?

It varies, but the average adult needs somewhere between seven and nine hours of sleep each night. The brain needs at least five sleep cycles of ninety minutes each to complete its full 'washing' cycle. Think of these like the cycles of a dishwasher. If you interrupt a dishwasher mid-wash, those dishes are going to come out dirty. Similarly, if you don't allow your brain to complete those five 90-minute cycles, your brain won't be as clear as it could be.

Sleep and appetite

Leptin and ghrelin – the hormones that regulate satiety and hunger (remember those from Chapter 5?) – are balanced while we sleep. And a lack of sleep can seriously mess with these hormones, which in turn makes you hungry, which makes you eat more, which makes you gain weight. On top of that, cortisol, the stress hormone, drops as we sleep. But if you don't get enough sleep, your cortisol levels stay high, and this can also affect your appetite and cause you to hold on to weight. On the plus side, you can actually burn calories while you sleep. Depending on your size and weight, you can burn somewhere between 50 and 100 or more calories per hour while snoozing – and even more if you're having a particularly stimulating dream.

Waking rest is just as important

Rest and sleep are very different things, but we need both of them. Resting restores us so we have energy to give to others. Restful activities include reading, meditating, going for a walk, journalling, watching TV or playing a board game. We all rest differently, so seek out leisure activities that make you feel grounded, restored, happy and revitalised.

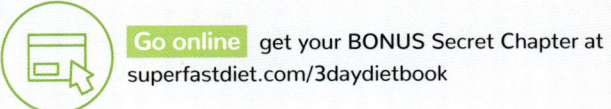

Go online get your BONUS Secret Chapter at superfastdiet.com/3daydietbook

Habit 5: Giving – AKA the life-changing magic of giving a f***

Too much has been made of not giving a f***. Granted, deciding on a list of the things in life that you do not care about can help you deal with anxiety and stress. But not giving a f*** about anything is just going to make you unhappy. People who give of themselves are generally happier.

If you flex your giving muscle a little by doing something nice for someone else – say volunteering for an organisation that means something to you or giving away one of your favourite books – you will feel good. Giving a f*** about other people is one of the secret keys to living an amazing life. Research shows that people who volunteer and donate their time tend to be happier, less stressed, less anxious and less prone to depression. They also experience better physical health and are more likely to live longer.

According to the University of Sydney, those who volunteer may also experience something known as a 'helper's high'. Volunteering triggers a reward pathway in the brain known as the mesolimbic system, which releases feel-good neurotransmitters such as oxytocin and vasopressin. So, caring about things, organisations and people isn't just good for the world, it's also *very* good for you!

Habit 6: Styling for success – time to shine

Styling is an important habit because the face you present to the world reflects your inner self. Discovering or changing your personal style (i.e. your hair, your makeup, your clothes) is a great way to let the world know that there's an amazing transformation taking place inside of you. Clothes allow you to embrace your confidence and individuality.

Let's start in your wardrobe. You'll want to cull any worn, tired and sad pieces to make way for shiny new ones that show off your new body so you can be your confident, stylish self. The average wardrobe looks like this:

- 20 per cent work clothes
- 15 per cent sweats and lounging-around clothes
- 50 per cent 'literally no one would look good in these' clothes
- 5 per cent 'I can't throw this out 'cos I had a great time in it once' clothes
- 5 per cent 'I can't believe I was ever this size' clothes
- 5 per cent 'everyone has seen me in this a million times, but it's one of the few things I like' clothes.

The good news is that your future is filled with shopping trips where you'll find stylish clothes that are more 'you', but you'll need to make space for them first. Aside from asking yourself whether each item sparks joy *a la* Marie Kondo, there are a few guidelines to help you decide whether to chuck something. It goes in the bin (or gets sold or donated) if it is …

- the wrong colour, the wrong size or hideously outdated
- a designer piece that you got for a steal (but don't actually wear)
- uncomfortable or something that requires constant adjusting
- a T-shirt from Munich Oktoberfest circa 1995, which still smells like beer.

If you have trouble letting go, at least make a separate pile to go through at a later date, but please don't keep them unless you actually wear them.

5 top tips to help you discover your style

1 Get inspired: Read magazines and blogs, pinning items and outfits you like. Look for common themes, like leopard print, neutral colours or 50s/60s/90s-inspired tailoring.

2 Develop a signature style: Seek out an aesthetic you love to become your signature look, whether that involves cute colourful socks, slicked-back hair or striking winged eyeliner.

3 Shop your closet: Mix and match pieces you have left with new items to create a refreshed look. Take the time to play with what you have and build new outfits.

4 Get a tailor on speed dial: Become BFFs with them and have your jeans hemmed and jacket darted so that everything fits you perfectly.

5 Dress for your shape: One of the best kept secrets of stylish people is that they know how to dress for their height and shape. Marilyn Monroe knew how to rock that hourglass silhouette; Kim Kardashian knows how to work her pear-shaped curves (she even broke the internet with them!); The Rock makes the most of his muscular physique by dressing in clean cuts and simple lines; and André Leon Talley, American *Vogue*'s editor-at-large, doesn't let the fact that he's 6'7" tall stop him from rocking whatever the heck he likes. So, how do you know which shape you are? Strip down to your skivvies and take a good look in the mirror. Where does your silhouette curve, where is it smaller and where is it larger?

Like health, style is a journey to enjoy! Try not to get bogged down in the rules – they're meant to help, not hinder. If all else fails, turn your style quest into a social activity by grabbing a few friends and taking on the shops, closet clean-out and outfit-planning sessions together.

Potential pitfalls

Elizabeth Gilbert, author of *Eat, Pray, Love* and *Big Magic* once said: 'Embrace the glorious mess that you are.' But it's not just us that's a glorious mess; *life* is a glorious mess! Life is jagged. Life is saying to yourself over and over, 'After this week, things will slow down a bit,' but that doesn't mean it isn't beautiful. In fact, those jagged, messy edges are part of what makes life beautiful. But here's the thing: sticking with a healthy lifestyle is *much* easier when life is smooth. At least, at first.

Anything new takes a little while to get used to, so until this 3-day diet becomes second nature (or at the very least for the first 66 days, which is how long researchers now believe it takes to embed a new habit), make it easier on yourself. Plan ahead for those messy, jagged moments where things are likely to become a little 'sh*t-showy' by putting in place a few simple strategies that will save you from stuff-ups.

Life is going to keep coming at you full speed, but the good news is that this 3-day diet is designed for life to happen around it. As you'll recall from previous chapters, it's flexible. So go with the flow. Crack the champagne if the occasion calls for it, go out for dinner if you're too tired to cook, but then wake up the next day and get back on track.

Remember, it's okay to fail. A comeback is often stronger than a setback. But why put yourself through a setback if you don't have to? In this chapter, you'll find some of our favourite solves for situations that are likely to trip you up and cause setbacks and stuff-ups. But first, let's talk about another F-word (no, not that one. And not fasting either – we covered that in Chapter 2, remember?). It's time to talk failure!

Newsflash: Failure isn't a dirty word

The problem with the modern perception of success is that we see failure as a bad thing. We don't want to fail. But here's the thing: you never win if you're so afraid of failure that you don't try. It's only by trying and failing that we learn life's valuable lessons. Robert Kiyosaki, author of *Rich Dad Poor Dad* and founder of Rich Global puts it this way: 'Winners are not afraid of losing. But losers are. Failure is part of the process of success. People who avoid failure also avoid success.'

People fail for a lot of reasons, but the main one (and perhaps the easiest one to address), is giving up too soon. Persistence, or 'stick-to-itiveness', as Thomas Edison called it, is often the key to success. The fact is most people fail primarily because they give up. So, what's the lesson? Don't give up. As Barack Obama said, 'The future rewards those who press on.'

Moving on from failure can be difficult, but it begins with acknowledging that you've failed, and then identifying *why* you failed, as well as what you can learn from the experience. Once you know why you've failed in the past, you can begin to see any patterns of self-sabotage or fear of failure. And being aware of something that's causing you to fail can be half the battle. Once you're aware of those negative patterns, you can start to watch out for them so you can change the way you think, and the way you approach things.

One of the most important things we ask people to do when they join our SuperFasters community is to complete an exercise that helps them examine why they've failed at diets in the past. And since you're reading this book, that makes you part of this club, so it's time for some self-examination. What negative patterns do you tend to repeat? Are you afraid of failure? Are you afraid of success? Do you have a tendency towards self-sabotage? Or are you, perhaps, surrounded by others who for their own self-interested or fearful reasons may prefer to see you fail? Only once you understand your patterns can you put better supports in place for yourself. The potential pitfalls should help you uncover a few of your patterns.

Meet Gin

BEFORE: 102.2 kg **AFTER:** 63.3 kg **KILOS GONE** 38.9 kg

Virginia used to joke that if you ever saw her running, you'd better start running yourself, because it meant something was chasing her. She never thought it was possible to lose weight without feeling deprived. But after kicking over 38 kilos, she's loving herself, loving life and discovering new passions ... including jogging!

'I loved the 3-day diet because, even on my fast days, I didn't feel like I was fasting! I was just making healthier choices. I could sit down with my family and eat the same dinner, because 1000 calories allowed me to do that. It taught me that you don't have to feel hungry to lose weight! It helped me learn how to eat healthier and how to replace my bad habits with good ones, but still be able to enjoy the foods I like. After losing over 38 kilos I had the confidence to change my career path. I have been feeling fitter, healthier and happier, and I now have a more positive outlook on life. I love walking and have even started jogging! SuperFastDiet is a way of life!'

Potential pitfall 1: Self-sabotage

Some of the other reasons that people fail, particularly at weight loss, have to do with deeper issues, and, consequently, self-sabotage often plays a role. Self-sabotage is any behaviour or action we take that gets in the way of us achieving our goals and becoming our best selves. Even though it can make us feel really bad, it's as if some untoward invisible force keeps moving us towards failure. Why? Well, there are a number of reasons we sabotage our chances to succeed.

- **Fear of failure:** Telling ourselves stories about unforeseen disasters, and tall tales about why things didn't (or can't) work out gives us a semblance of control. And that's something which actual failure can't provide.
- **Fear of success:** Success means change, and change is scary! Fear of success is often associated with low self-worth. We tell ourselves 'I don't deserve this,' or that we're not fit to succeed ... so we don't.
- **Procrastination:** We defer starting something because it's boring or too hard.
- **Setting the bar too high:** We make success impossible by making our goals too big or too complex.
- **We feel safer staying the same:** Sometimes we'd rather stay where we are, even if that means being miserable, than embrace the possibility of change and the unknown. Because, once again, change is scary!

Strategies to overcome self-sabotage

Embrace change and give yourself a real chance at success by trying some of these strategies for overcoming self-sabotage.

- Be realistic about what you're able to achieve right now.
- Set small, achievable goals (see page 40).
- Be patient: you'll get there!
- Be kind to yourself.
- Expect setbacks.
- Celebrate every win.

Ultimately, self-sabotage is something we can all overcome. Like many things, the secret lies in being kind to ourselves, as well as – at the same time – challenging ourselves to be the best possible person we can be. We're not going to lie: it's a tough balance, but it IS possible. And it IS worth it.

Potential pitfall 2: Comfort eating and bingeing

When we comfort eat, we eat more than we should, we tend to eat unhealthily, and we don't properly process the negative emotions that have caused the comfort eating in the first place. Food makes us feel good, at least for a little while. And because this behaviour makes us feel better, we tend to do it again and again.

Repeated behaviours are more likely to become established and self-reinforcing. And as you've just learned, it takes 66 days for a new habit to form. That can feel like a lifetime when you're trying to establish more challenging habits, like going for a run first thing in the morning. But when it comes to enjoyable behaviours, like eating, those 66 days can go by in a flash! Not only are these behaviours bad for your waistline, they also stop you from properly processing your emotions. Stuffing feelings down or covering them over with food means we don't take the time to feel or understand why they're there in the first place. And though you may feel better in the short term, those emotions are likely to bubble back again. It's a vicious cycle!

Strategies to overcome comfort eating and bingeing

Granted, not all emotions are fun to feel. Regret, sadness, anger, rage and even less intense emotions like jealousy or guilt can be very unpleasant. But you feel those emotions for a reason, and you need to take the time to properly process them. Below are some helpful strategies you can use to begin overcoming comfort eating and bingeing. But please note: If binge eating or emotional eating is really getting you down or goes on for too long, please seek professional medical help from someone experienced in this area.

- **Be mindful of your emotions.** Take time to objectively assess how you feel. Journal or write about them if it helps to work through your feelings.
- **If you notice an urge to comfort yourself with food, ask yourself, 'What am I craving specifically?'** Then ask, 'What am I feeling? What feeling or situation am I trying to escape?'
- **Get comfortable being uncomfortable.** Dr. Tim Sharp is a psychologist and author of *Live Happier, Live Longer*, as well as one of the experts on our award-winning online program. He says, 'An important, but often neglected aspect of happiness is accepting and getting used to being unhappy. We don't always have to "fix" unpleasant emotions.'
- **Write a list of alternative, more helpful behaviours.** For example, riding out the emotion, journalling, chatting to a friend or going for a walk.

Potential pitfall 3: Failing to prepare

You know that old saying, 'fail to plan, plan to fail'? Well, it's true! We're never our best selves when we're tired, emotional, stressed, time-poor, overstretched or juggling more than one or two things at once. But these times are unavoidable, and it's during these times that we're likely to find ourselves scrambling for healthy choices and instead turning to whatever food is available. But overcoming potential obstacles is heavily reliant on our ability to spot them before they arise. There are two components to doing this:

1 **Actually spotting said obstacle.**

2 **Spotting said obstacle in enough time to do something constructive about it.**

There are definitely going to be times when you don't have any food prepared – this is a very common potential stuff-up. And unfortunately, malls, food courts and hangry feels just don't mix with healthy goals. But that doesn't mean you have to resort to faceplanting into a cheeseburger.

Strategies to be more proactive

When you are feeling like your best self (well rested, calm, well fed and thinking clearly), take time to think ahead and write down any situations that have the potential to set you back. How might 'old you' react to these situations? By reaching for a drink? Eating too much? Giving up? Now, think of ways you could side-step those obstacles and stay on track. For example, if you've got a weekday social event coming up and you think it's likely to trip you up, perhaps you can move one of your 'on days' to the weekend? Taking a proactive approach is incredibly worthwhile and it will make your transition to the 3-day diet lifestyle so much smoother and so much more effortless.

And on those crazy days when you haven't had time to prepare, we've compiled a list of fast food that won't sabotage your efforts on the scales. Snap a pic of the page opposite on your phone and use it to help you navigate those wobbly moments.

Our fave fast food feast day options

FAST FOOD OUTLET	GOOD OPTION	OTHER OPTIONS
KFC	**Original Fillet Burger** (396 calories)	**Zinger Burger** (high in protein and only 425 calories)
McDonalds	**Grilled Chicken Salad, no dressing** (196 calories) **Hamburger** (252 calories)	**Filet-o-fish** (338 calories) **Grilled Chicken Clubhouse** (523 calories) **McFeast** (534 calories)
Oporto	**Single Fillet Bondi Burger** (416 calories and lowest fat content)	**Chicken Taca Bowl** (429 calories and high in protein)
A corner shop	**Grilled steak and salad sandwich or a grilled chicken burger** (about 400–500 calories)	1 BBQ chicken thigh and 2 cups of salad (270 calories)
Domino's Pizza	**Penne pasta with roasted chicken, mushrooms and vine-ripened tomatoes** (404 calories)	4 slices thin crust Vegorama pizza (556 calories)
Subway	**Veggie Delite Salad** (61 calories)	**Veggie Delite 6-inch sub** (211 calories)
Red Rooster	**The Classic Roast** (509 calories)	**Roast Veg Medley** (299 calories)
Guzman Y Gomez	**Mild Pulled Pork Salad without dressing** (222 calories)	**Naked Pan Seared Barramundi Bowl** (673 calories)
Sushi	**Fresh sashimi and seaweed salad** (379 calories)	Miso soup, no additions (35 calories)

The 3-Day Diet

Potential pitfall 4: Funky feels

We all have down days where we feel blue, overwhelmed or just plain 'over it'. Whether you woke up on the wrong side of the bed or didn't get enough sleep, or you're dealing with some real-life issues that are causing you stressy feels, chances are you'll have to navigate some not-so-great days while you're on this diet. But we've got some ideas for you.

Strategies to overcome funky feels

Thankfully, there are many constructive things we can do to help pull ourselves out of the doldrums.

- **Write a list of things you're grateful for:** Gratitude is like armour against funky feels.
- **Move it:** Go for a walk, dance around the house or do some squats.
- **Get outside:** Fresh air, nature and the great outdoors is an ideal way to reset.
- **Meditate or be mindful:** Anything that draws you into the present moment will help to reset your mood.
- **Cuddle up:** Physical touch releases the feel-good hormone oxytocin.
- **Talk it out:** Call your BFF, mum or nana and have a good old natter.
- **Laugh it off:** This is where our earlier recommendation for YouTube comes in. Cat videos! 'Nuff said.
- **Do something new:** Nothing changes your perspective like a new experience, whether that's dinner somewhere new, a walk somewhere you've never been or a movie you've never seen before.
- **Get nostalgic:** Look through photos or read journal entries from happier times.
- **Do something for someone else:** Giving and kindness release oxytocin and dopamine, two of nature's most powerful antidepressants.
- **Treat yo'self:** A small indulgence can make you feel better, from a tiny square of dark chocolate to a lavish bubble bath.
- **Get wet:** Take a swim, take a shower or wash your face. Not only is self-care soothing, being around water optimises your respiration, encouraging oxygen towards the heart and brain. (That's why we often have great ideas or revelations in the shower.)

Prepare for the dreaded plateau

It is an unfortunate fact of weight loss that you will hit a plateau at some stage. In fact, you may hit more than one plateau over the course of your weight loss. It's common to hit a plateau at around the 12-week mark, then perhaps again somewhere around the 18 to 24 week mark. But don't fret! It is possible to overcome a plateau by employing the following tactics:

- **Recalculate your TDEE:** Once you lose weight, you're a smaller human being, which means you burn fewer calories. Recalculating your TDEE and basal metabolic rate is a surefire way to kick your weight loss back into top gear for a second whoosh!
- **Start exercising:** It doesn't have to be much, just one 20-minute walk per day can help shift those last few kilos, and it's fantastic for your mental health. In fact, one of the most intensive, long-term studies of intermittent fasting recently confirmed that exercise or any kind of movement was critical to ensuring long-term weight maintenance post weight loss.
- **Take another look at what you're eating:** One of the ways to approach a plateau can be to go back to basics like weighing your food, being careful about your portion sizes and re-reading some of the most inspiring sections of this book. Take a second look at how many calories are in the foods you're eating; maybe you've been guesstimating or maybe your portions have gotten a little out of control.
- **Set new goals:** There's nothing like a brand new goal to re-motivate you for a second swing at the scales. A short-term mini-goal can work wonders!
- **Take some time off:** Sometimes it can do you good to take some time off of a healthy-eating plan. Good food, with zero other associations, is good for your mental health and for your soul.

10 super-good-mood foods

Each one of these ingredients has been scientifically proven to either improve mood or decrease the risk of depression. Incorporate these mood-boosters into your diet as often as you can and let them work their natural magic on you today, tomorrow and into the future.

1 Turmeric

2 Coffee

3 Berries

4 Oily fish
such as salmon, mackerel and tuna

How to stay on track, no matter what!

The great thing about the 3-day diet is that it's an approach you can always come back to, no matter what because a) it works and b) it's easy, so it's a long-term solution that will keep you slim and healthy forever. And this is great news for you. So this next part is a crash course in how to get it done, get it over with and not need us anymore.

Kick those last five kilos

The last three-to-five kilos are always the hardest to shift, and the easiest to gain. If you find yourself struggling with them, here are a few things you can do to get rid of them (or get rid of them *again*).

- **Rethink your stress levels:** Having high cortisol levels is one of the greatest weight-loss saboteurs. So if you find yourself regaining weight, especially if you're working a lot, it's time to rethink your schedule. Aim to get more sleep, more exercise and reduce stress wherever you can. Be kind to yourself. You're doing the best you can.
- **Consider resistance training:** Anything you can do to build muscle mass will assist you in burning more fat even when you're doing nothing. You don't have to start going to the gym; resistance training can be as simple as lifting a two-litre bottle of milk twenty times a few times a week.
- **Ditch the drink:** You'll be surprised (or horrified!) by how many calories are in alcohol. If you're really struggling to lose the last few kilos, then something like Dry July can be a nice reminder of how little you really need alcohol. Enjoy that clear-headed feeling, enjoy how much better you sleep and, chances are, you'll see results on the scales too.
- **Tune in to your emotions:** If you're really struggling with the last few kilos, then check in with yourself. Are you eating mindlessly or comfort eating? This tends to happen on 'off days' more often than it happens on 'on days'. When you find yourself feeling bummed out or tired, notice what it is that you reach for.

Adjust the IF methods to maintain your weight

Once you reach your goal, it's often necessary to adjust the methods slightly to suit your new weight and slender figure. Here are the steps we suggest.

1. Gradually increase your calorie intake from 1000 calories per day (or 50 per cent of your calorie needs) to 1400 calories per day (or 70 per cent of your daily calorie needs) on your 'on days'. If you find yourself gaining weight, you can always return to 1000 calories per day.

2. If you're not already incorporating 16:8 into your routine, this might be the time to start – either with or without calorie counting as a maintenance program. Many of our SuperFasters find that this is a great everyday solution.

3. Move to incorporate strength-building exercises and cardio into your workout. Aim to exercise every day – brisk walking is fine. The optimum is 45 minutes a day, but if you can only swing 20 minutes, that's better than nothing. Just keep moving!

4. Watch less television! We know it sounds strange, but while watching television we are bombarded with food commercials, which prompts us to snack more.

5. Weigh yourself at least once a week so you can catch any minor slip-ups and stop them in their tracks before they become bigger ones.

There are so many approaches when it comes to weight maintenance. It's up to you to find what works for you – ultimately, something that's easy to stick to and can be easily slotted into your daily life is going to be the best and most sustainable approach. Sticking to the principles of good nutrition you've been working on throughout your weight-loss journey will also keep you on track.

Eat balanced, nutritious meals and remember, don't drink your calories!

CHAPTER 7

The recipes

Food, glorious food

The following is not your average recipe section ... au contraire, these next pages hold the key to your great success on the 3-day diet.

Start by checking out the staples – these brilliant basics pack a flavoursome, super-low-cal punch to any dish and will save you SO much time.

Then simply make up your three fast days (of 1000 calories) by choosing:

☐ **One breakfast (200 calories)**

☐ **One lunch (300 calories)**

☐ **One dinner (400 calories)**

☐ **Snack or dessert (100 calories)**

How easy is that! We've done the calorie counting for you.

The breakfast and lunch options have deliberately been designed to be quick and portable so you can take them with you anywhere.

Feel free to mix it up however you wish. For instance, if you don't want to eat breakfast and want to eat within an eight-hour window, simply go straight to lunch and trade those brekkie calories for an extra snack or add the suggested calorie boosters. Or plan whatever food or drinks you like in your day and simply account for those calories.

STAPLES

Drizzles and dressings

Tamari–ginger drizzle

Makes approx. 1 cup * Serves approx. 6 (2 tablespoons)
* Prep 10 minutes * Cals per serve (2 tablespoons) 47 * Vegan

½ cup (125 ml) tamari
¼ cup (60 ml) mirin
finely grated zest and juice of 2 limes
1 tablespoon finely grated ginger

Place the ingredients in a screw-top jar and season with pepper. Put the lid on tightly, then shake vigorously to combine. Use or store in an airtight container in the fridge for up to 1 week, shaking before use.

Notes

- This versatile drizzle can be used as a marinade, dressing or dipping sauce. Drizzle it wherever you want added flavour.
- You will need a 4 cm piece of peeled ginger to produce 1 tablespoon grated ginger.

Thyme-ly mustard dressing

Makes approx. 1 cup * Serves approx. 6 (2 tablespoons)
* Prep 10 minutes * Cals per serve (2 tablespoons) 35 * Vegan

1 tablespoon extra virgin olive oil
½ cup (125 ml) red wine vinegar
⅓ cup dijon mustard
2 tablespoons fresh thyme leaves, chopped

Place the ingredients in a screw-top jar and season with pepper. Put the lid on tightly, then shake vigorously to combine. Use or store in an airtight container in the fridge for up to 1 week, shaking before use.

Note

- You can swap the fresh thyme for 1 teaspoon dried thyme leaves.

Creamy dollop

Makes 1½ cups * Serves 9 (2 tablespoons)
* Prep 15 minutes * Cook 2 minutes + cooling
* Cals per serve (2 tablespoons) 40 * Vegan

1 tablespoon brown mustard seeds
1 tablespoon cumin seeds
1 cup (250 g) natural coconut yoghurt
1 garlic clove, crushed
finely grated zest and juice of 1 large lemon

Place the mustard and cumin seeds in a small non-stick frying pan over low heat. Cook, shaking the pan occasionally, for 1–2 minutes until the mustard seeds start to pop and the mixture smells fragrant. Transfer to a bowl and leave to cool.

Add the remaining ingredients to the bowl, whisk well and season with pepper. Use or store in an airtight container in the fridge for up to 1 week, stirring before use.

Virtually no-cal-gal dressing

Makes ¾ cup * Serves 9 (1 tablespoon)
* Prep 15 minutes * Cals per serve (1 tablespoon) 7 * Vegan

finely grated zest and juice of 1 large lemon
¼ cup (60 ml) apple cider vinegar
2 teaspoons wholegrain mustard
½ teaspoon dried mixed herbs
pinch of powdered stevia (optional)

Put the ingredients in a screw-top jar and season with pepper. Screw the lid on tightly, then shake vigorously to combine. Use or store in an airtight container in the fridge for up to 1 week, shaking before use.

Staples

Basic veggie paste

Get this paste prepped and raring to go for stress-free, quick weeknight meals. This perfect flavour base will save you chopping and grating every night!

Makes 4 cups * Serves 8 (½ cup)
* Prep 20 minutes
* Cals per serve (½ cup) 27 * Vegan

1 onion, roughly chopped
2 garlic cloves
2 celery stalks, roughly chopped
3 carrots, roughly chopped
2 zucchini, roughly chopped
½ small bunch flat-leaf parsley, cut into 5 cm lengths
2 tablespoons red wine vinegar
1 tablespoon sea salt

Put the ingredients in a large food processor and process until smooth (adding 1–2 tablespoons water to help, if needed). Use or store in an airtight container in the fridge for up to 1 week, stirring occasionally, or in the freezer for up to 3 months. Defrost in the fridge overnight.

Note

- This mixture naturally changes colour slightly when it is stored in the fridge or freezer.

Basic spice paste

Prep this spice paste for the week ahead to add to your favourite Asian-flavoured meals – and make your weekdays way easier (and spicier)!

Makes 1¾ cups * Serves 7 (¼ cup)
* Prep 15 minutes
* Cals per serve (¼ cup) 11 * Vegan

1 red onion, roughly chopped
2 garlic cloves
3 long green chillies, roughly chopped
5 cm piece ginger, peeled and halved
1 small bunch coriander, cut into 5 cm lengths
1 tablespoon apple cider vinegar
1 tablespoon sea salt

Place the ingredients in a food processor and process until smooth. Use or store in an airtight container in the fridge for up to 1 week, stirring occasionally, or in the freezer for up to 3 months. Defrost in the fridge overnight (the coriander will discolour slightly on defrosting).

Notes

- There is minimal heat in long green chillies; however, if you're concerned, you can simply remove the seeds to reduce any heat, or leave out the chillies completely (deduct 1.5 calories per ¼ cup serve).
- This mixture naturally changes colour slightly when it is stored in the fridge or freezer.

Basic dried spice blend

Makes 2¼ cups * Serves 27 (1 tablespoon)
* Prep 5 minutes
* Cals per serve (1 tablespoon) 18 * Vegan

25 g jar ground cumin
20 g jar ground coriander
24 g jar ground cardamom
25 g jar ground ginger
35 g jar sweet paprika
50 g jar garlic powder
40 g jar onion powder

Empty the contents of each jar into a large bowl. Whisk together until well combined. Use or store in an airtight container in your pantry for up to 3 months.

Note

- Use the empty spice jars to store your dried spice blend. Mark the labels with the new recipe name and date it was made.

The 3-Day Diet

Staples

Recipe basics

Vegelicious tomato sauce

Need pizza sauce? Pasta sauce? Ketchup? Passata? Enjoy this all-purpose and delicious home-made tomato sauce in your next family feast ... without the nasties.

Makes approx. 6 cups (1.5 litres) * Serves 6 (1 cup)
* Prep 20 minutes * Cook 40 minutes
* Cals per serve (1 cup) 90 * Vegan

- 1 tablespoon extra virgin olive oil
- 1 red onion, coarsely grated
- 2 garlic cloves, crushed
- 2 zucchini, coarsely grated
- 2 celery stalks, finely chopped
- 2 carrots, coarsely grated
- 140 g tomato paste
- 2 x 400 g cans whole peeled tomatoes
- ½ teaspoon dried mixed herbs
- 2 small vegetable stock cubes

Heat the oil in a large saucepan over medium heat and add the onion, garlic, zucchini, celery and carrot. Cook, partially covered and stirring occasionally, for 15 minutes or until very soft and starting to colour. Add the tomato paste. Cook, stirring, for 1 minute.

Add the canned tomatoes, herbs, stock cubes and ½ cup (125 ml) water. Cook, stirring and breaking up the tomatoes with the back of a spoon, until the mixture comes to a simmer.

Reduce the heat to low, partially cover the pan and cook, stirring occasionally, for 20 minutes or until the mixture has reduced by half and thickened. Season with pepper and leave to cool slightly. Use or store in an airtight container in the fridge for up to 1 week or in the freezer for up to 6 months. Defrost in the fridge overnight.

Note
- Younger family members might prefer a smoother sauce; if so, cool the mixture and then blend until smooth in the saucepan with a hand-held stick blender.

Gluten-free muesli

Makes 13 cups (800 g) * Serves 26 (½ cup)
* Prep 15 minutes * Cook 15 minutes + cooling
* Cals per serve (½ cup) 141 * Vegan

- 165 g mixed seeds (pumpkin seeds, sunflower seeds)
- 120 g flaked almonds
- 2 teaspoons ground cinnamon
- 1 teaspoon ground nutmeg
- 260 g gluten-free corn flakes
- 250 g gluten-free rice puffs

Preheat the oven to 180°C (160°C fan-forced). Line a baking tray with non-stick baking paper. Combine the seeds, almonds, cinnamon and nutmeg in a bowl, then spread evenly over the tray in a single layer.

Bake for 10–12 minutes until golden. Cool completely on the tray, then transfer to a large bowl. Add the corn flakes and rice puffs, tossing together well.

Store in an airtight container in your pantry for up to 1 month.

Herbaceous vegetable broth

Give this nourishing veggie-packed broth a go for the perfect extra-low-cal fast day filler! You can even whip this up as a staple to add to any recipe that calls for stock to be used. We love saving money and cutting down on those preservatives! #winwin

Makes approx. 3 litres ∗ **Serves approx.** 12 (1 cup)
∗ **Prep** 40 minutes ∗ **Cook** 2 hours 10 minutes + 1 hour cooling
∗ **Cals per serve** (1 cup) 9 ∗ **Vegan**

- 1 tablespoon extra virgin olive oil
- 4 onions, unpeeled but skins washed, ends trimmed, quartered
- 6 garlic cloves, halved
- 6 tomatoes, quartered
- 8 carrots, cut into 3 cm lengths
- ½ bunch celery, cut into 3 cm lengths
- 8 zucchini, cut into 3 cm lengths
- 2 small bunches flat-leaf parsley, cut into 3 cm lengths
- 1 bunch thyme
- 1 bunch oregano
- 4 stalks rosemary
- 1 tablespoon sea salt

Heat the oil in a large stockpot over medium heat. Add the onion and cook, stirring occasionally, for 7 minutes or until starting to soften. Add the garlic and cook, stirring, for 2 minutes or until fragrant.

Add the remaining ingredients, then cover with 5 litres water. Cook, stirring occasionally, until it comes to the boil. Reduce the heat to a simmer.

Simmer for 2 hours, partially covered and stirring occasionally, or until the vegetables have completely collapsed and the liquid reduced by a quarter (if you find the liquid is evaporating too quickly, top up with extra water and reduce the heat further). Remove the pan from the heat, mash the vegetables roughly and then leave, covered, for 1 hour.

Strain the vegetable broth very well, pressing down on the vegetables to extract as much liquid as possible. Discard the solids. Use immediately or store in airtight containers in the fridge for up to 1 week or the freezer for up to 6 months. Defrost in the fridge overnight.

Note

- If you don't own a large stockpot, simply divide the ingredients into two extra-large saucepans instead.

The 3-Day Diet

200
CALORIE

BREAKFASTS

Breakfast

Filling toast toppers

There are a lot of different sandwich thins available on supermarket shelves, so use a range to keep your food interesting and delicious. Sandwich thins are designed to be split in half.

Lemon–pepper ricotta and salmon

Serves 1 • Prep 10 minutes • Cals per serve 138

Combine 2 tablespoons fresh ricotta, 2 teaspoons lemon juice and ¼ teaspoon black pepper. Spread over ½ toasted wholemeal sandwich thin. Top with 50 g drained flaked canned red salmon, 1 teaspoon finely grated lemon zest and ¼ cup baby rocket leaves. Season and serve.

Ham and capsicum melt

Serves 1 • Prep 10 minutes • Cook 2 minutes • Cals per serve 184

Top ½ toasted wholegrain sandwich thin with 25 g sliced reduced-fat ham, 1 piece (20 g) roasted capsicum and 15 g sliced reduced-fat Swiss cheese. Cook under a hot grill for 1–2 minutes until the cheese melts. Season and serve topped with 2 tablespoons baby rocket leaves.

Lemon–pepper ricotta and salmon

Breakfast

Marinated mushrooms

Serves 1 • Prep 10 minutes + 20 minutes standing • Cals per serve 123 • Vegan

Thinly slice 100 g button mushrooms, then toss with 2 tablespoons Thyme-ly mustard dressing (page 112). Marinate for 20 minutes, stirring occasionally. Top ½ toasted wholegrain sandwich thin with ¼ cup baby spinach leaves, then top with the marinated mushroom and 1 teaspoon toasted pumpkin seeds. Season and serve.

Hummus, tomato and feta

Serves 1 • Prep 10 minutes • Cals per serve 192 • Vegetarian

Spread ½ toasted wholemeal sandwich thin with 2 tablespoons hummus, 1 slice of tomato and ¼ cup small basil leaves. Crumble 25 g reduced-fat Greek feta over the top, season and serve.

Herb and tomato omelette

Serves 1 • Prep 10 minutes • Cook 2 minutes • Cals per serve 149 • Vegetarian

Heat a non-stick frying pan over medium–high and spray lightly with olive oil cooking spray. Add 1 whisked egg to the pan, swirling to coat the base and form a thin omelette. Immediately sprinkle with 1 tablespoon finely chopped chives, 1 tablespoon finely chopped parsley and 1 tablespoon dill leaves. Cook, untouched, for 1–2 minutes or until set firm. Remove the pan from the heat and scatter with 50 g sliced cherry tomatoes. Fold the omelette in half to enclose the tomato and herbs, then fold in half again. Top ½ toasted sandwich thin with the omelette. Season and serve.

Hummus, tomato and feta

Marinated mushrooms

Veggie-boosted scrambles for one

Tomato and mushroom egg scramble

Serves 1 • Prep 10 minutes • Cook 5 minutes • Cals per serve 131 • Vegetarian

Heat a non-stick frying pan over medium–high heat and spray lightly with olive oil cooking spray. Add 1 chopped tomato, 100 g sliced button mushrooms and 1 sliced spring onion and cook, stirring, for 2 minutes to soften slightly. Add 1 whisked egg and scramble for 1–2 minutes until set. Remove from the heat and stir in ¼ cup baby spinach leaves until just wilted. Season and serve.

Turmeric capsicum tofu scramble

Serves 1 • Prep 10 minutes • Cook 5 minutes • Cals per serve 100 • Vegan

Heat a non-stick frying pan over medium–high heat and spray lightly with olive oil cooking spray. Add 1 small chopped red capsicum, ½ thinly sliced red onion and ½ teaspoon ground turmeric and cook, stirring, for 2 minutes to soften slightly. Add 100 g silken tofu and break it up as you scramble for 2–3 minutes, or until heated through and light golden. Remove from the heat and stir in ¼ cup baby rocket leaves. Season and serve.

Garlic mushroom and pea egg scramble

Serves 1 • Prep 10 minutes • Cook 5 minutes • Cals per serve 151 • Vegetarian

Heat a non-stick frying pan over medium–high heat and spray lightly with olive oil cooking spray. Add 200 g sliced mixed mushrooms (Swiss brown, oyster, button) and 1 small crushed garlic clove. Cook, stirring, for 3 minutes to soften slightly. Add 1 whisked egg and ¼ cup frozen baby peas and scramble for 1–2 minutes until set. Remove from the heat and stir in 1 tablespoon thyme leaves. Season and serve.

Zucchini and kale egg scramble

Serves 1 • Prep 10 minutes • Cook 5 minutes • Cals per serve 117 • Vegetarian

Heat a non-stick frying pan over medium–high heat and spray lightly with olive oil cooking spray. Add 1 sliced zucchini and 1 torn kale leaf and cook, stirring, for 3 minutes to soften slightly. Add 1 whisked egg and 2 tablespoons finely chopped chives and scramble for 1–2 minutes until set. Remove from the heat and stir in the finely grated zest and juice of ½ small lemon. Season and serve.

Roast veggie tofu scramble

Serves 1 • Prep 15 minutes • Cook 20 minutes • Cals per serve 127 • Vegetarian

Preheat the oven to 200°C (180°C fan-forced). Line a baking tray with non-stick baking paper. Arrange 100 g chopped butternut pumpkin, 50 g quartered brussels sprouts and ½ chopped red onion on the tray. Spray lightly with olive oil cooking spray and roast for 15 minutes or until cooked and golden. Heat a non-stick frying pan over medium–high heat. Spray lightly with olive oil cooking spray. Add 1 small crushed garlic clove, 2 teaspoons finely chopped rosemary and 100 g silken tofu. Break up the tofu as you scramble for 2–3 minutes, or until heated through and light golden. Remove from the heat and stir in the roast veggies. Season and serve.

Garlic mushroom and pea egg scramble

Turmeric capsicum tofu scramble

Breakfast

Ginger blueberry

Page 124

Ham, corn and feta

Page 125

Ricotta spinach
Page 125

Raspberry cheesecake ripple
Page 125

Choc-banana
Page 124

Lemon poppy seed
Page 125

Breakfast

Marvellous breakfast muffins

We caught your eye with muffins, didn't we? Muffins can be the perfect way to start your day when done the 3-day diet way! Whether you are more of a savoury stan or a sweet tooth, we have got you covered for an easy on-the-run, nutritionally packed brekkie treat.

Basic muffin recipe

Makes 12 ∗ Prep 15 minutes ∗ Cook 20 minutes
∗ Cals per serve (1 muffin) 145 ∗ Vegan

2 cups (320 g) wholemeal self-raising flour
2 teaspoons baking powder
1 teaspoon powdered stevia
½ cup (125 g) unsweetened apple puree
¼ cup (60 ml) macadamia oil
¾ cup (180 ml) unsweetened rice milk

Step 1: Preheat the oven to 190°C (170°C fan-forced). Line a 12-hole, ⅓ cup capacity muffin tray with paper cases.

Step 2: Stir together the flour, baking powder and stevia in a large bowl. Make a well in the centre.

Step 3: Combine the apple puree, oil, rice milk and ¼ cup (60 ml) water and pour into the well in the dry ingredients. Fold together with a large metal spoon until just combined and sticky looking; do not overmix or the muffins will be tough.

Step 4: Spoon into the paper cases in the muffin tray. Bake for 20 minutes, or until golden and cooked through when tested with a skewer. Leave in the tray for 3 minutes before transferring to a wire rack. Serve warm or at room temperature.

Notes

- Use this Basic muffin recipe as your base to then add in your fave flavour combos.
- Cooled muffins can be stored in an airtight container in your pantry for up to 3 days.

Ginger blueberry

Cals per serve (1 muffin) 157 ∗ Vegan

Stir 60 g fresh blueberries + 2 teaspoons ground ginger + an additional 2 tablespoons powdered stevia into the flour mixture in step 2.

Add 2 teaspoons vanilla extract to the apple puree mixture in step 3.

Sprinkle the muffins with 60 g blueberries before baking, pressing them gently into the mixture.

Choc–banana

Cals per serve (1 muffin) 159 ∗ Vegetarian

Stir 1 chopped firm banana + 2 tablespoons sugar-free drinking chocolate into the flour mixture in step 2.

Add 2 teaspoons vanilla extract to the apple puree mixture in step 3.

Sprinkle the muffins with 2 teaspoons sugar-free drinking chocolate before baking.

Ricotta spinach

Cals per serve (1 muffin) 159 * **Vegetarian**

Pour boiling water over 60 g baby spinach leaves until wilted, then drain and rinse under cold running water. Place in a clean tea towel and wring dry, then finely chop.

Stir the spinach into the flour mixture in step 2 with 100 g crumbled fresh ricotta + 1 thinly sliced spring onion.

Sprinkle the muffins with 1 thinly sliced spring onion before baking, pressing it gently into the mixture.

Ham, corn and feta

Cals per serve (1 muffin) 191

Stir 200 g crumbled reduced-fat Greek feta + the kernels cut from 1 corn cob + 50 g finely chopped reduced-fat ham + 1 small, finely chopped bunch chives into the flour mixture in step 2.

Sprinkle the muffins with 50 g finely chopped reduced-fat ham before baking.

Raspberry cheesecake ripple

Cals per serve (1 muffin) 161* **Vegetarian**

Add 2 teaspoons vanilla extract to the apple puree mixture in step 3.

Process ¾ cup frozen raspberries + 50 g extra-light cream cheese + 2 tablespoons powdered stevia in a small food processor until smooth. Fold gently through the mixture after folding in the apple puree mixture, to create a ripple effect.

Lemon poppy seed

Cals per serve (1 muffin) 155 * **Vegan**

Stir 2 tablespoons poppy seeds + 2 tablespoons finely grated lemon zest + an additional 2 tablespoons powdered stevia into the flour mixture in step 2.

Add 2 tablespoons lemon juice + 2 teaspoons vanilla extract to the apple puree mixture in step 3.

Breakfast

Rainbow veggie rosti with avocado, tomatoes and dukkah

Serves 4 | Prep 30 minutes | Cook 20 minutes | Cals per serve 173 | Vegetarian

No, you absolutely don't need to head down to the local cafe to get yourself a winning brunch pic – simply whip together this rainbow rosti. This gorgeous meal is full of healthy fats and plenty of fabulous fibre. For a protein hit, add an egg for just 80 calories extra.

1 avocado, sliced
200 g cherry tomatoes, halved lengthways
⅓ cup (80 ml) **Thyme-ly mustard dressing** (page 112)
1 zucchini, coarsely grated
300 g peeled, seeded and coarsely grated Kent pumpkin
2 carrots, coarsely grated
1 egg yolk
1 small bunch chives, thinly sliced
olive oil cooking spray
⅓ cup (75 g) hummus
1 tablespoon pistachio dukkah
fresh herbs and lemon wedge, to serve (optional)

Gently toss together the avocado, tomato and Thyme-ly mustard dressing in a bowl. Season and set aside.

Wrap the grated zucchini in a clean tea towel and ring dry, then transfer to a bowl. Stir in the pumpkin, carrot, egg yolk and chives. Season well.

Heat a large non-stick frying pan over medium–high heat and spray lightly with oil. Divide the mixture into eight, and spoon four portions into the pan, shaping into rounds and pressing down firmly until each round is about 1 cm thick. Cook for 4–5 minutes each side until cooked and golden. Remove from the pan and cook the remaining four rosti.

Serve the rosti with the hummus and the tomato mixture, and sprinkle with dukkah and herbs, if using, and a lemon wedge, if using.

Family additions Serve with fried, hard-boiled or poached eggs and thick buttered toast.

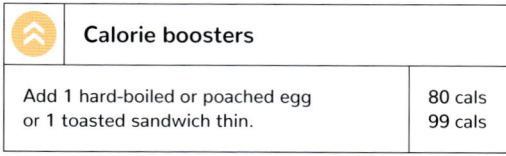

Calorie boosters	
Add 1 hard-boiled or poached egg or 1 toasted sandwich thin.	80 cals 99 cals

Breakfast

Gluten-free muesli and raspberry parfaits

Serves 4 **Prep** 15 minutes **Cals per serve** 173 **Vegan**

Are you after something a little 'cafe-esque' without the fuss? Enter our fabulously fruity parfait. We love this sweet four-ingredient mix that is both gluten-free and vegan. The perfect parfait, you might say!

1 cup (250 g) natural coconut yoghurt
2 teaspoons pure maple syrup
250 g fresh raspberries, torn in half
1 cup (60 g) **Gluten-free muesli** (page 114)

Gently fold together the yoghurt, syrup and most of the raspberries (keep a few for serving) in a bowl.

Spoon half the Gluten-free muesli into four serving glasses, top with half the raspberry mixture, then the remaining muesli and then the remaining raspberry mixture. Sprinkle the reserved raspberries on top to serve.

Family additions Add extra yoghurt, raspberries and maple syrup, or sliced banana or peaches. Sprinkle with toasted flaked coconut.

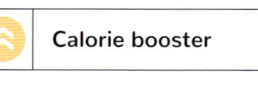

	Calorie booster	
	Add 2 teaspoons toasted flaked coconut.	30 cals

Breakfast

Full breakfast tray bake

Serves 4   Prep 25 minutes   Cook 30 minutes   Cals per serve 197

For the perfect weekend brunch to satisfy the whole family, you can't go past this wholesome spread, full of colour and a whole lot of essential vitamins and minerals. Your body will be thanking you after this one!

olive oil cooking spray
250 g peeled, seeded and chopped Kent pumpkin
2 zucchini, chopped
6 roma tomatoes, halved lengthways
2 teaspoons **Basic dried spice blend** (see page 113)
100 g reduced-fat shaved ham
50 g reduced-fat sliced Swiss cheese
1 green capsicum, deseeded, sliced into 4 thick rings
4 eggs

Preheat the oven to 200°C (180°C fan-forced). Lightly spray a large non-stick baking tray with oil.

Place the pumpkin, zucchini and tomato (cut-side up) on the tray. Sprinkle with the Basic dried spice blend, then spray lightly with oil. Roast for 15 minutes or until starting to soften.

Top each tomato half with ham, and then cheese. Add the capsicum rings to the tray, making sure they are sitting flat. Crack an egg into each capsicum ring. Season, then spray lightly with oil. Return to the oven for 5–7 minutes until the egg whites have set and the yolks are slightly runny or cooked to your liking. Take the tray straight to the table to serve.

Family additions Serve with avocado wedges and thick buttered toast or add extra eggs to the tray.

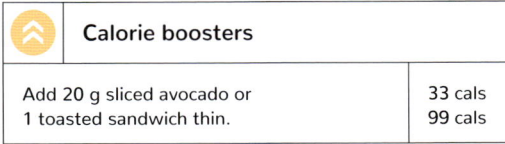

Calorie boosters	
Add 20 g sliced avocado or	33 cals
1 toasted sandwich thin.	99 cals

Breakfast

Apple cranberry bircher

Serves Prep Cals per serve Vegetarian
4 15 minutes + 174
  chilling overnight

Getting your day going with the goodness of oats is one of the best things you can do! Prep this brekkie the night before to start your day off on the right foot. Yes, you cran!

1½ cups (135 g) rolled oats
1½ cups (375 ml) reduced-sugar cranberry juice
2 teaspoons natural vanilla extract
½ teaspoon ground cardamom
½ teaspoon ground ginger
1 small red apple, coarsely grated
½ cup (125 g) non-fat plain Greek yoghurt
1 tablespoon toasted pumpkin seeds

Stir together the oats, juice, vanilla, spices and apple in an airtight container. Refrigerate overnight.

Stir in the yoghurt. Divide among small bowls or glasses and serve sprinkled with pumpkin seeds.

Family additions Serve topped with extra yoghurt, sliced banana, a spoonful of nut butter and a drizzle of honey or pure maple syrup.

Calorie boosters	
Add ½ sliced banana,	46 cals
¼ cup Greek yoghurt or	30 cals
1 tablespoon toasted pecans.	45 cals

300
CALORIE

LUNCHES

Lunch

Substantial sandwich fillings

Curried chickpeas

Serves 1 * Prep 15 minutes * Cals per serve 256 * Vegan

Using a fork, mash together ⅓ cup rinsed, well-drained canned chickpeas, 2 teaspoons korma curry paste, 2 tablespoons **Creamy dollop** (page 112) and 2 tablespoons finely chopped chives. Layer inside a wholegrain sandwich thin with 1 cup shredded iceberg lettuce and ½ grated carrot. Season and serve.

Salmon and nutty cream cheese

Serves 1 * Prep 15 minutes * Cals per serve 249

Combine 2 teaspoons extra-light cream cheese, the finely grated zest and juice of ½ small lemon and 1 teaspoon finely chopped toasted pine nuts. Spread over the inside of 1 wholegrain sandwich thin, then top with 50 g drained flaked canned red salmon, 1 Lebanese cucumber peeled into thin strips and ½ cup baby salad leaf mix (baby spinach and baby rocket). Season and serve.

Beef and beetroot hummus

Serves 1 * Prep 15 minutes * Cook 1 minute * Cals per serve 245

Preheat a non-stick frying pan over high heat. Quickly fry 50 g seasoned beef sizzle steaks for 30 seconds each side until just cooked and golden. Layer inside a burger thin with 2 tablespoons beetroot hummus, 1 tablespoon finely sliced red onion, 2 thinly sliced baby cucumbers and ½ cup firmly packed baby rocket leaves. Season and serve.

Curried chickpeas

Salmon and nutty cream cheese

Lunch

Egg nicoise

Serves 1 * Prep 15 minutes
* Cals per serve 241 * Vegetarian

Spread 1 tablespoon olive tapenade over the inside of a wholemeal sandwich thin. Top with 1 cup shredded baby cos lettuce leaves, then 50 g steamed baby green beans and 1 halved hard-boiled egg. Drizzle with 1 teaspoon red wine vinegar. Season and serve with parsley leaves.

Prawn cocktail

Serves 1 * Prep 15 minutes
* Cals per serve 159

Top 1 wholegrain sandwich thin with 1 cup shredded iceberg lettuce. Stir together 2 teaspoons **Creamy dollop** (page 112), 1 teaspoon reduced-sugar tomato ketchup and 1 tablespoon dill leaves. Combine with 50 g chopped cooked prawn meat, then spoon over the lettuce. Season and serve with a lemon wedge.

Chicken Waldorf

Serves 1 * Prep 15 minutes
* Cals per serve 286

Combine 50 g chopped skinless BBQ chicken breast meat, 1 finely chopped celery stalk, 2 finely chopped walnuts, 1 thinly sliced spring onion, ½ small red apple, cut into matchsticks and 1 tablespoon **Creamy dollop** (page 112). Layer inside a wholemeal sandwich thin with 2 thickly shredded baby cos lettuce leaves and ¼ cup flat-leaf parsley leaves. Season and serve.

Egg nicoise

Prawn cocktail

Beef and beetroot hummus

Chicken Waldorf

Creamy pumpkin with crunchy cumin chickpeas

Page 138

Prawn tom yum

Page 139

Hearty zucchini, kale and quinoa

Page 138

Make-ahead freeze-able soups

Hearty veggie and chicken soup

Serves 4 * Prep 25 minutes * Cook 15 minutes
* Cals per serve 246

Combine 6 cups (1.5 litres) **Herbaceous vegetable broth** (page 115), 2 chopped carrots, 2 chopped baby fennel, 2 chopped zucchini, 300 g peeled and chopped butternut pumpkin, 400 g chopped chicken breast, 2 tablespoons rosemary leaves and 2 tablespoons thyme leaves in a large saucepan over medium heat. Simmer, partially covered and stirring occasionally, for 15 minutes or until cooked. Season and serve, or store in an airtight container.

Hearty zucchini, kale and quinoa

Serves 4 * Prep 20 minutes * Cook 15 minutes
* Cals per serve 144 * Vegan

Combine 6 cups (1.5 litres) **Herbaceous vegetable broth** (page 115), 4 sliced zucchini, 4 sliced celery stalks, 2 crushed garlic cloves and 100 g quinoa in a large saucepan over medium heat. Simmer, partially covered and stirring occasionally, for 15 minutes or until cooked. Remove from the heat and stir in 2 shredded kale leaves and the finely grated zest and juice of 1 lemon. Season and serve, or store in an airtight container.

Creamy pumpkin with crunchy cumin chickpeas

Serves 4 * Prep 30 minutes * Cook 20 minutes
* Cals per serve 193 * Vegetarian

Cook 400 g well-rinsed canned chickpeas and 2 teaspoons cumin seeds in a large non-stick frying pan over high heat for 2–3 minutes until crisp and golden. Set aside.

Combine 6 cups (1.5 litres) **Herbaceous vegetable broth** (page 115), 2 chopped zucchini, 2 garlic cloves and 800 g peeled and chopped butternut pumpkin in a large saucepan over medium heat. Simmer, partially covered and stirring occasionally, for 15 minutes or until cooked. Cool slightly and stir in 2 tablespoons non-fat plain Greek yoghurt. Season and blend until smooth. Store in an airtight container, or top with the crunchy cumin chickpeas and serve immediately.

Spiced carrot and cauliflower

Serves 4 * Prep 20 minutes * Cook 15 minutes
* Cals per serve 76 * Vegan

Combine 6 cups (1.5 litres) **Herbaceous vegetable broth** (page 115), 4 chopped carrots, 500 g cauliflower florets, 2 crushed garlic cloves and 1 tablespoon **Basic dried spice blend** (page 113) in a large saucepan over medium heat. Simmer, partially covered and stirring occasionally, for 15 minutes or until cooked. Cool slightly, then blend until smooth. Season and serve, or store in an airtight container.

Beans and greens

Serves 4 * **Prep** 25 minutes * **Cook** 10 minutes
* **Cals per serve** 209 * **Vegan**

Combine 4 cups (1 litre) **Herbaceous vegetable broth** (page 115), 2 cups (500 ml) **Vegelicious tomato sauce** (page 114), 400 g drained canned four-bean mix, 300 g halved green beans and 1 bunch shredded silverbeet leaves in a large saucepan over medium heat. Simmer, partially covered and stirring occasionally, for 10 minutes or until cooked. Season and serve, or store in an airtight container.

Prawn tom yum

Serves 4 * **Prep** 25 minutes * **Cook** 10 minutes
* **Cals per serve** 131

Combine 6 cups (1.5 litres) **Herbaceous vegetable broth** (page 115), ¼ cup **Basic spice paste** (page 113), 4 chopped tomatoes, 4 torn kaffir lime leaves and 400 g raw prawn meat in a large saucepan over medium heat. Simmer, partially covered and stirring occasionally, for 10 minutes or until cooked. Remove from the heat and stir in 100 g baby spinach leaves, 2 shredded spring onions, 100 g shredded snow peas and the juice of 1 lime. Season and serve, or store in an airtight container.

Storing notes Always cool soup to room temperature before pouring into airtight containers.

Soups can be kept in the fridge for up to 3 days and in the freezer for up to 3 months. Always defrost in the fridge overnight.

Lunch

Rolls that rock

Sashimi sushi rolls

Serves 1 • Prep 15 minutes • Cals per serve 300

Combine 80 g finely chopped sashimi salmon, 80 g diced avocado and 1 cup shredded rainbow salad mix. Divide between 2 nori sheets, roll up tightly into logs and secure the ends with a little water. Serve with 2 lime wedges.

Tuna omelette roll

Serves 1 • Prep 15 minutes + cooling • Cook 2 minutes • Cals per serve 286

Whisk together 2 eggs and 1 thinly sliced spring onion. Heat a non-stick frying pan over high heat and spray lightly with olive oil cooking spray. Pour in the egg mixture, swirling to coat the base. Cook, untouched, for 2 minutes or until set firm. Slide out of the pan and onto a plate. When cool, top with ½ cup baby spinach leaves, 100 g drained flaked tuna in springwater, ½ cup baby rocket leaves and 1 tablespoon **Virtually no-cal-gal dressing** (page 112). Season. Fold in the sides, then roll up tightly into a log. Cut in half and serve with a lemon wedge.

Curried-egg mountain bread roll

Serves 1 • Prep 15 minutes • Cals per serve 297 • Vegetarian

Mash together 2 hard-boiled eggs, 1 teaspoon curry powder and 2 tablespoons **Creamy dollop** (page 112). Spoon down one side of a spelt mountain bread, then top with ½ cup shredded iceberg lettuce, ¼ cup coarsely grated carrot and 50 g snow pea sprouts. Season and roll up into a log. Cut in half to serve.

Mushroom fajita lettuce rolls

Serves 1 • Prep 20 minutes • Cook 5 minutes • Cals per serve 105 • Vegan

Heat a large non-stick frying pan over high heat and spray lightly with oil. Cook 200 g sliced mixed mushrooms (Swiss brown, portobello, button), 2 sliced spring onions, 1 sliced small red capsicum and 1 tablespoon **Basic dried spice blend** (page 113) for 5 minutes or until softened. Cool slightly, then spoon into 3 iceberg lettuce leaf cups. Roll up tightly into logs. Serve with 2 lime wedges.

Rice paper tofu rolls

Serves 1 • Prep 20 minutes • Cals per serve 295 • Vegan

Dip 1 large rice paper round into tepid water to soften slightly. Lay flat, then top with 1 cup baby salad leaf mix, 100 g sliced firm tofu and ½ cup coriander leaves. Fold in the sides, then roll up tightly into a log. Cut in half and serve with 1 tablespoon **Tamari–ginger drizzle** (page 112) for dipping.

Chicken Caesar mountain bread roll

Serves 1 • Prep 15 minutes • Cals per serve 286

Combine 75 g chopped skinless BBQ chicken breast meat, 1 tablespoon shaved parmesan, 2 tablespoons **Creamy dollop** (page 112) and 1 tablespoon finely chopped chives. Spoon down one side of a spelt mountain bread, then top with 3 torn baby cos lettuce leaves and 50 g sliced cherry tomatoes. Season and roll up into a log. Cut in half to serve.

Lunch

Chicken Caesar mountain bread roll

Sashimi sushi rolls

Rice paper tofu rolls

Lunch

Make-ahead salads

Deconstructed falafel salad

Serves 1 * Prep 15 minutes * Cals per serve 258 * Vegan

Combine ¾ cup well-rinsed canned chickpeas, ½ cup flat-leaf parsley leaves, ½ cup mint leaves, ½ cup basil leaves, 2 thinly sliced spring onions, 2 chopped tomatoes, 1 chopped Lebanese cucumber and 2 tablespoons **Thyme-ly mustard dressing** (page 112) in an airtight container. Season and chill overnight.

Egg and soba noodle salad

Serves 1 * Prep 15 minutes * Cals per serve 296 * Vegetarian

Combine ½ cup cooked soba noodles, 2 halved hard-boiled eggs, 100 g steamed baby green beans, 2 thinly sliced celery stalks, ½ thinly sliced red capsicum and 2 tablespoons **Tamari–ginger drizzle** (page 112) in an airtight container. Season and chill overnight.

Deconstructed falafel salad

142

Lunch

Prawn rice salad

Serves 1 * **Prep** 15 minutes * **Cals per serve** 282

Combine ⅓ cup cooked brown basmati rice, 100 g chopped cooked prawn meat, ½ finely chopped green capsicum, ½ cup coarsely grated carrot, 2 thinly sliced spring onions and 2 tablespoons **Virtually no-cal-gal dressing** (page 112) in an airtight container. Season and chill overnight.

Prawn rice salad

Egg and soba noodle salad

Lunch

Tofu couscous salad

Serves 1 ✱ Prep 20 minutes ✱ Cals per serve 291 ✱ Vegan

Soak 2 tablespoons wholemeal couscous and 1 teaspoon harissa paste in ⅓ cup boiling water for 10 minutes until the water has been absorbed and the couscous is tender. Combine with 50 g chopped firm tofu, 4 thinly sliced baby red radishes, 2 thinly sliced celery stalks, 3 thinly sliced baby cucumbers and 1 small peeled and thinly sliced naval orange in an airtight container. Season and chill overnight.

Roast potato salad

Serves 1 ✱ Prep 15 minutes + cooling ✱ Cook 15 minutes ✱ Cals per serve 262 ✱ Vegan

Preheat an oven to 200°C (180°C fan-forced). Line a baking tray with non-stick baking paper. Arrange 200 g halved unpeeled baby potatoes, 100 g peeled and chopped butternut pumpkin and 1 chopped red onion on the tray and spray lightly with olive oil cooking spray. Season and roast for 15 minutes or until cooked through and golden. Cool on the tray, then combine with 100 g steamed baby green beans, ¼ cup flat-leaf parsley leaves and 2 tablespoons **Thyme-ly mustard dressing** (page 112) in an airtight container. Season and chill overnight.

Tamari chicken and veggie salad

Serves 1 ✱ Prep 15 minutes ✱ Cals per serve 258

Combine 100 g chopped skinless BBQ chicken breast, 125 g zucchini noodles, 50 g thinly baby corn halved lengthways, ½ cup bean sprouts, ½ finely sliced green capsicum, 2 shredded spring onions and 2 tablespoons **Tamari–ginger drizzle** (page 112) in an airtight container. Season and chill overnight.

Roast potato salad

Lunch

Tamari chicken and veggie salad

Tofu couscous salad

400 CALORIE

DINNERS

Dinner

Super bowls

Korma chickpea and freekeh bowls

Serves 4 * Prep 30 minutes * Cook 20 minutes * Cals per serve 370 * Vegetarian

100 g freekeh
½ cup **Basic veggie paste** (page 113)
1 tablespoon korma curry paste
2 x 400 g cans chickpeas, rinsed well
1 cup (250 ml) **Herbaceous vegetable broth** (page 115)
50 g baby spinach leaves
400 g broccoli florets, steamed
½ cup coriander leaves, to serve

Cook the freekeh in a large saucepan of boiling water for 20 minutes or until just tender. Drain, then refresh under cold running water. Drain well and set aside.

Meanwhile, stir together the Basic veggie paste, korma paste, chickpeas and Herbaceous vegetable broth in a saucepan over medium heat. Simmer, stirring occasionally, for 15 minutes or until reduced by half. Season.

Arrange the spinach in serving bowls, then top with the broccoli, freekeh and chickpea mixture. Sprinkle with coriander to serve.

Family additions Serve with Greek yoghurt, toasted naans and mango chutney.

Moroccan pumpkin and couscous bowls

Serves 4 * Prep 15 minutes + 10 minutes standing * Cook 20 minutes * Cals per serve 196 * Vegan

500 g peeled, seeded and diced Kent pumpkin
2 zucchini, cut into thick matchsticks
2 tablespoons **Basic dried spice blend** (page 113)
olive oil cooking spray
½ cup (100 g) wholemeal couscous
¾ cup (180 ml) **Herbaceous vegetable broth**, heated (page 115)
1 teaspoon harissa paste
100 g baby rocket
¼ cup pomegranate seeds
1 tablespoon toasted flaked almonds

Preheat the oven to 200°C (180°C fan-forced). Line a large baking tray with non-stick baking paper. Arrange the pumpkin and zucchini on the tray and sprinkle with the Basic dried spice blend, then spray with oil. Toss to combine and coat well. Bake for 20 minutes, or until cooked and golden.

Meanwhile, combine the couscous, Herbaceous vegetable broth and harissa in a bowl, cover and leave for 10 minutes, or until the couscous softens and all the liquid has been absorbed.

Arrange the rocket in serving bowls, add the couscous and top with the roast pumpkin mixture. Sprinkle with pomegranate seeds and almonds to serve.

Family additions Add chopped firm tofu to the tray before baking the vegetables, and serve with extra toasted flaked almonds.

Calorie boosters	
Serve with 1 tablespoon plain Greek yoghurt or ½ toasted wholemeal naan.	54 cals 115 cals

Calorie boosters	
Add an extra 1 teaspoon toasted flaked almonds.	10 cals

Dinner

Garlic chicken and quinoa bowls

Serves 4 * **Prep** 20 minutes * **Cook** 15 minutes * **Cals per serve** 245

4 garlic cloves, crushed
2 tablespoons tamari
400 g chicken tenderloins, halved crossways
1 bundle (3 pieces) baby bok choy, quartered lengthways
½ cup (100 g) quinoa
400 g snow peas, trimmed
2 spring onions, shredded
coriander leaves and lime wedges, to serve (optional)

Combine the garlic, tamari, chicken and baby bok choy in a bowl and marinate.

Cook the quinoa in a saucepan of boiling water over high heat for 15 minutes, or until cooked. Stir in the snow peas and then drain well.

Preheat a large chargrill pan over high heat. Chargrill the chicken mixture in 2 batches, for 5–7 minutes each batch, or until the chicken is cooked through and golden and the bok choy wilted.

Spoon the quinoa into serving bowls and top with the chicken and bok choy. Sprinkle with spring onion and coriander, if using, and serve with a lime wedge, if using.

`Family additions` Increase the quinoa and chicken per serve and add fresh baby corn to the chargrill.

Calorie boosters	
Add 50 g fresh baby corn to the chargrill.	15 cals

The 3-Day Diet

Dinner

Tandoori salmon and barley bowls

Serves 4 * **Prep** 20 minutes + 5 minutes resting * **Cook** 35 minutes * **Cals per serve** 255

½ cup (100 g) barley
¼ cup non-fat plain Greek yoghurt
2 tablespoons finely chopped mint
4 x 120 g skinless boneless salmon fillets
1 tablespoon tandoori paste
1 bunch English spinach, leaves torn
2 Lebanese cucumbers, finely chopped
1 small red onion, finely chopped
½ cup coriander leaves

Cook the barley in a saucepan of boiling water for 30–35 minutes until tender. Drain, then refresh under cold running water.

Combine the yoghurt and mint in a bowl and chill until required.

Meanwhile, preheat an oven grill to high. Place the salmon on a non-stick baking tray and brush all over with the tandoori paste. Cook under the grill for 8 minutes, turning carefully only once. Leave to cool for 5 minutes before flaking into large pieces. Cover to keep warm.

Place the spinach in a colander and pour boiling water over it until wilted. Drain well.

Combine the cucumber and onion in a bowl and season.

Spoon the barley, salmon and spinach into serving bowls. Top with the cucumber mixture and yoghurt mixture. Sprinkle with coriander to serve.

Family additions Increase the barley and salmon per serve.

Calorie boosters	
Add 100 g chopped eggplant to the tray before grilling the salmon.	25 cals

Black bean and pulse pasta bowls

Serves 4 * **Prep** 10 minutes * **Cook** 10 minutes * **Cals per serve** 294 * **Vegan**

¾ cup (100 g) pulse pasta
400 g can black beans, rinsed well
1½ cups (375 ml) **Vegelicious tomato sauce** (page 114)
4 large kale leaves, stalks discarded, leaves torn
¼ cup toasted mixed seeds (pumpkin seeds, sunflower seeds)
½ cup small basil leaves
25 g snow pea sprouts

Cook the pasta in a saucepan of boiling water over high heat for 8–10 minutes until just cooked. Drain and refresh under cold running water.

Meanwhile, place the beans, Vegelicious tomato sauce and kale in a saucepan over medium heat. Simmer for 10 minutes or until the kale is wilted and the sauce reduced by half.

Spoon the pasta and bean mixture into bowls. Top with the seeds, basil leaves and sprouts to serve.

Family additions Increase the pulse pasta and black beans per serve.

Calorie boosters	
Add 1 chopped zucchini to the bean mixture in step 2.	33 cals

Dinner

Beef and wild rice bowls

Serves 4 * **Prep** 20 minutes * **Cook** 10 minutes * **Cals per serve** 267

½ cup (100 g) wild rice
200 g lean beef stir-fry strips
400 g baby green beans
1 tablespoon smoked paprika, plus extra to serve
olive oil cooking spray
2 baby cos lettuces, leaves separated
2 carrots, coarsely grated
1 avocado, sliced
1 lime, cut into wedges
coriander leaves, to serve (optional)

Cook the rice in a saucepan of boiling water over high heat for 25–30 minutes until cooked. Drain well.

Meanwhile, combine the beef, beans and smoked paprika in a bowl and spray with oil.

Heat a large non-stick wok over high heat. Stir-fry the beef mixture in 3 batches, for 4 minutes each batch, or until just cooked and golden.

Spoon the rice into serving bowls. Add the beef mixture and top each bowl with cos, carrot and avocado. Sprinkle with extra paprika and coriander, if using, and serve with lime wedges.

Family additions Increase the rice and beef per serve and add edamame.

Calorie boosters

Add ¼ cup podded steamed edamame.	63 cals

Dinner

Astounding apricot chicken capsicums

Serves
4

Prep
15 minutes +
15 minutes standing

Cook
50 minutes

Cals per serve
309

Capsicums add crunch and sweetness to your dinner. When you stuff them with apricot chicken, a true family favourite, you have got yourself a real winner, winner chicken dinner.

6 large green capsicums, halved lengthways, stalks and seeds removed
½ cup (100 g) wholemeal couscous
2 tablespoons **Basic dried spice blend** (page 113)
400 g chicken breast stir-fry strips
410 g can apricot halves in natural juice
mixed salad greens, to serve

Preheat the oven to 190°C (170°C fan-forced). Line a baking dish with non-stick baking paper. Put the capsicum halves in the dish, cut-side up.

Stir together the couscous and Basic dried spice blend in a large bowl. Season. Stir in the chicken, then the whole can of apricots and juice. Leave for 10 minutes, stirring occasionally.

Spoon the apricot-chicken mixture evenly into the capsicum halves. Cover with a piece of non-stick baking paper, then cover the entire dish with foil. Bake for 30 minutes, then uncover and bake for a further 20 minutes, or until the chicken is cooked, the couscous tender and the capsicum halves golden.

Leave to rest for 3 minutes before serving with mixed salad greens.

Family additions Serve with steamed green beans and toasted sourdough.

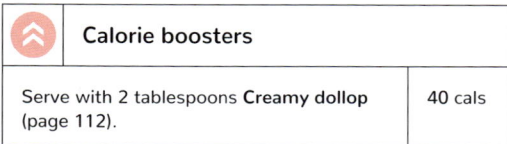

⇧	Calorie boosters	
Serve with 2 tablespoons **Creamy dollop** (page 112).		40 cals

152   The recipes

Dinner

Chicken and spinach dahl

Serves	Prep	Cook	Cals per serve
4	10 minutes + 5 minutes standing	30 minutes	311

Dahl, you need to try this! Sorry, we couldn't help ourselves. This dish boasts over 30 g of protein per serve. Simply swap out the chicken for chickpeas to make it meat-free.

½ cup **Basic spice paste** (page 113)
1 tablespoon **Basic dried spice blend** (page 113)
400 g diced chicken breast
1 cup (200 g) split red lentils
2 small vegetable stock cubes, crumbled
1 bunch English spinach, leaves torn
1 lime, cut into halves
½ cup coriander leaves

Heat a large saucepan over medium heat. Add the Basic spice paste and Basic dried spice blend and cook, stirring, for 2 minutes until fragrant. Add the chicken and cook, stirring occasionally, for 5 minutes, or until just starting to colour.

Stir in the lentils, stock cubes and 4 cups (1 litre) water. Bring to a simmer, then reduce the heat to medium–low. Simmer gently, partially covered and stirring occasionally, for 18–20 minutes, or until the chicken is cooked, the lentils have broken down and the mixture has thickened.

Remove from the heat and stir in the spinach. Leave covered for 5 minutes until the spinach wilts. Season and stir well. Serve with lime wedges and coriander.

Family additions Serve with poppadoms, toasted naan, mango chutney and raita.

Calorie boosters	
Serve with microwaved mini poppadoms	32 cals
or top with 2 tablespoons raita.	30 cals

Dinner

Spiced chicken breast and veggie tray bake

Serves 4   Prep 20 minutes + 5 minutes standing   Cook 30 minutes   Cals per serve 373

Everyone loves a one-pan-cooks-all type of dinner: less cleaning and a whole lot of deliciousness! This tray bake is full of colour, flavour and nutrition, with the perfect mix of healthy carbs (our favourite), gorgeous veggies and beautifully spiced chicken.

- 4 x 120 g chicken breast fillets
- 400 g baby green beans, trimmed
- 300 g mixed baby tomatoes, halved
- 1 red onion, cut into wedges
- 500 g baby potatoes, unpeeled, halved
- 2 tablespoons **Basic dried spice blend** (page 113)
- 2 tablespoons red wine vinegar
- olive oil cooking spray

Preheat the oven to 200°C (180°C fan-forced). Line a large baking tray with non-stick baking paper.

Toss together the chicken, beans, tomato, onion, potato, spice blend and vinegar in a large bowl until well combined. Spread evenly over the tray, making sure the chicken breasts aren't covered by any vegetables. Season, then spray with oil.

Bake for 25–30 minutes until cooked through, turning the chicken and vegetables twice. Leave to rest for 5 minutes before taking the whole tray to the table to serve.

Family additions Serve with extra baby potatoes and crumbled Danish feta.

Calorie boosters	
Add 25 g crumbled Danish feta to serve.	66 cals

Dinner

Slow-cooker five-spice chicken

Serves	Prep	Cook	Cals per serve
4	10 minutes	4 hours	227

Get those tastebuds dancing with this fragrant slow-cooked chook. Pop it on in the morning and come home to the ultimate no-fuss winter warmer. Serve with cauliflower rice or jasmine rice, depending on if it is a fast day or not (or who you are sharing with!).

½ cup **Basic spice paste** (page 113)
3 teaspoons five-spice powder
400 g chicken breast fillets
2 tablespoons tamari
125 g baby corn, halved lengthways
2 bundles (6 pieces) baby bok choy, halved lengthways
2 spring onions, thinly sliced diagonally

Preheat a slow cooker on High. Put the spice paste, five-spice powder, chicken, tamari and 1½ cups (375 ml) water in the slow cooker. Cover and cook for 4 hours, turning the chicken twice during cooking.

Add the corn and bok choy and cook, covered, for another 20 minutes or until the greens wilt.

Shred the chicken breasts with 2 forks and stir through the vegetables. Spoon into serving bowls and sprinkle with spring onion to serve.

Note
- 400 g is 1–2 chicken breasts, depending on the size you purchase.

Family additions Serve with cooked jasmine rice and toasted cashews.

Calorie booster	
Serve with ½ cup cooked jasmine rice or top with 1 tablespoon chopped toasted cashew nuts.	120 cals 49 cals

Dinner

Impossible chicken, feta and chive quiche

Serves
4

Prep
15 minutes +
5 minutes standing

Cook
50 minutes

Cals per serve
393

It is hard to go wrong with this deliciously nutritious quiche. Packed to the brim with a whole lot of protein, enjoy right away, or freeze for a quick dinner to pull out during the week!

olive oil cooking spray
½ cup (75 g) plain flour
2 cups (500 ml) reduced-fat milk
4 eggs
2 tablespoons olive oil
200 g chopped skinless **BBQ chicken breast**
1 small bunch chives, finely chopped
100 g reduced-fat Greek feta, crumbled
mixed green salad, to serve

Preheat the oven to 180°C (160°C fan-forced). Lightly spray a deep 20 cm glass pie plate with oil.

Place the flour in a large bowl and make a well in the centre. Whisk together the milk, eggs and oil in a large jug. Season and pour into the well, whisking until smooth. Stir in the chicken, chives and half the feta. Pour into the pie plate and sprinkle with the remaining feta. Season.

Bake for 45–50 minutes until set firm and golden. Leave to rest for 5 minutes, then slice and serve with salad.

Note

- Make it vegetarian by swapping out the chicken for a mix of some of your favourite veggies such as capsicum, mushrooms and pumpkin!

Family additions Serve with garlic bread and extra Greek feta.

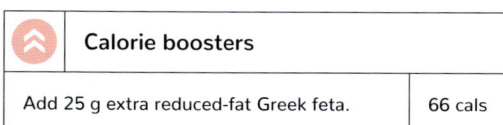

Calorie boosters	
Add 25 g extra reduced-fat Greek feta.	66 cals

The recipes

Dinner

Greek chicken meatballs and Zeus salad

Serves 4 | Prep 25 minutes | Cook 15 minutes | Cals per serve 247

Take your tastebuds to the Med with this stunning Greek-inspired dish. It's easy to whip together this meatball and salad combo on a weeknight, and it results in delicious lunch leftovers. It is so good you'll want to smash the plate … opa!

- 500 g chicken mince
- 1 egg yolk
- ¼ cup panko breadcrumbs
- 50 g reduced-fat Greek feta, crumbled
- 1 tablespoon finely chopped oregano
- finely grated zest and juice of 1 large lemon
- olive oil cooking spray
- 300 g mixed baby tomatoes, quartered
- 50 g pitted Kalamata olives, chopped
- 1 small iceberg lettuce, cored, cut into 5 cm pieces
- ½ cup small mint leaves

Using clean hands, mix together the mince, yolk, panko, feta, oregano and lemon zest in a large bowl. Season, then shape into 16 meatballs, using around 1 heaped tablespoon of mixture for each ball.

Heat a large non-stick frying pan over medium–high heat. Spray well with oil. Add the meatballs, spraying the tops with a little more oil. Cook for 10–12 minutes, turning occasionally, until cooked and golden. Remove from the heat and leave to stand for 3 minutes.

Toss together the tomato, olives, lettuce, mint and lemon juice. Season, then arrange on serving plates. Top with the meatballs to serve.

Family additions Add boiled, cooled potatoes to the salad mixture and serve with extra Greek feta and toasted sourdough.

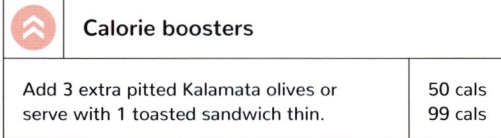

Calorie boosters	
Add 3 extra pitted Kalamata olives or serve with 1 toasted sandwich thin.	50 cals 99 cals

Dinner

Curried chicken and mango magic salad

Serves 4 | Prep 15 minutes | Cook 15 minutes | Cals per serve 260

Who said fruit doesn't belong in a salad? Never, ever us! We are (almost) famous for our 'super salads', which combine fruit with greens and colourful veg, plus of course a lovely lean protein. Hence why the addition here of gorgeous summery mango makes us swoon.

400 g chicken tenderloins, halved
1 red onion, cut into thin wedges
3 teaspoons curry powder
olive oil cooking spray
1 cos lettuce, cut into 3 cm pieces
100 g baby rocket leaves
2 Lebanese cucumbers, sliced
1 bunch baby red radishes, sliced into rounds
1 large mango, peeled and diced (400 g mango flesh)
1 tablespoon toasted flaked almonds
2 limes, halved

Toss together the chicken, onion and curry powder in a bowl. Season, then spray lightly with oil. Preheat a large chargrill pan over medium heat.

Chargrill the chicken and onion together for 10–12 minutes, turning occasionally, until cooked and golden. Transfer to a large bowl and leave to cool for 5 minutes.

Add the cos, rocket, cucumber, radish and mango to the bowl and toss gently together. Arrange the salad on serving plates and sprinkle with almonds. Serve with lime halves.

Note
- You will need a large mango; an RTE2 variety is the perfect size.

Family additions Add shaved parmesan and chopped toasted macadamias, and serve with toasted Turkish bread.

Calorie booster	
Add 2 teaspoons shaved parmesan or	15 cals
1 tablespoon chopped, toasted macadamia nuts.	55 cals

The 3-Day Diet

Dinner

Sweet chilli prawns with crunchy noodle salad

Serves
4

Prep
20 minutes

Cook
10 minutes

Cals per serve
102

We love this decadent salad for the perfect 'doesn't feel like a fast day' meal, plus the fact that it can so easily be bulked up for other family members. Add in some soba noodles or top it with some delicious roasted peanuts and boom – everyone is happy!

400 g raw prawn meat
¼ cup (60 ml) **Tamari–ginger drizzle** (page 112)
1 long red chilli, finely chopped
2 teaspoons pure maple syrup
1 red onion, cut into thin wedges
olive oil cooking spray

Crunchy noodle salad
500 g zucchini and carrot noodles
2 cups (200 g) bean sprouts
2 Lebanese cucumbers, cut into matchsticks
1 cup coriander leaves
1 cup small basil leaves
2 tablespoons **Tamari–ginger drizzle** (page 112)

Combine the prawns, Tamari–ginger drizzle, chilli, syrup and onion in a bowl. Season.

Make the crunchy noodle salad by combining the ingredients in a large bowl.

Heat a large non-stick wok over high heat. Spray with oil and add half the prawn mixture. Stir-fry for 2–3 minutes until cooked, golden and dry. Transfer to a bowl and stir-fry the remaining prawn mixture.

Serve the crunchy noodle salad in bowls, topped with the stir-fried prawns.

Note
- You can leave the prawn mixture to marinate for up to 24 hours in step 1; store in an airtight container in the fridge.

Family additions Add cooked soba noodles and chopped roasted peanuts to the salad.

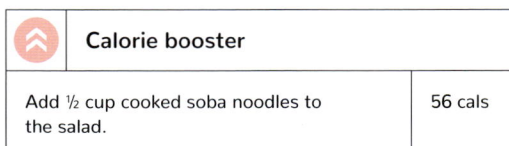

Calorie booster	
Add ½ cup cooked soba noodles to the salad.	56 cals

Dinner

Prawny fried rice

Serves 4   **Prep** 15 minutes   **Cook** 10 minutes   **Cals per serve** 164

Prawns are our all-time favourite protein source in the SFD office, being one of the best bangs for your calorie-buck. We squeezed those calories down even further by using cauliflower rice, one of our fave go-to savvy swaps for the perfect fast day wok up!

olive oil cooking spray
2 eggs, whisked
400 g raw prawn meat
3 spring onions, sliced, plus 1 extra to serve
½ cup (65 g) frozen baby peas
1 red capsicum, finely chopped
125 g baby corn, sliced into rounds
500 g cauliflower rice
2 tablespoons **Tamari–ginger drizzle** (page 112)

Heat a large non-stick wok over high heat and spray with oil. Add the egg, season and scramble in the wok for 1 minute until just set. Transfer to a bowl.

Reheat the wok over high heat. Spray with oil, add the prawn meat, season and stir-fry for 2 minutes. Add the spring onion, peas, capsicum and corn and stir-fry for 1 minute. Add the cauliflower rice and Tamari–ginger drizzle and stir-fry for 2 minutes until cooked and dry.

Remove from the heat and toss the egg through the rice. Serve in bowls, sprinkled with the extra sliced spring onion.

Note

- If you don't have a wok, use a large non-stick frying pan instead.

Family additions Serve with cooked jasmine rice and add chopped toasted cashews.

Calorie booster	
Add 1 teaspoon chopped toasted cashew nuts or ½ cup cooked brown rice.	50 cals 108 cals

The 3-Day Diet

Dinner

Charming chargrilled barramundi with cauli mash and creamy lemon sauce

Serves 4 | Prep 15 minutes | Cook 15 minutes | Cals per serve 243

The three components of this restaurant-worthy recipe are simply a match made in heaven. Better yet, it only takes up 30 minutes of your evening. The lemon sauce adds a zesty taste sensation to complement the healthy mash and the brilliant barra. Voila!

600 g cauliflower florets
400 g peeled potato, diced into 1 cm cubes
1 small chicken stock cube, crumbled
4 x 120 g skinless boneless barramundi fillets
2 bunches asparagus, trimmed and halved

Creamy lemon sauce
¼ cup (60 ml) **Thyme-ly mustard dressing** (page 112)
finely grated zest and juice of 1 small lemon
1 tablespoon non-fat plain Greek yoghurt
lemon wedges and flat-leaf parsley leaves, to serve (optional)

Make the creamy lemon sauce by combining the ingredients in a jug. Season and refrigerate until required.

Put the cauliflower, potato and stock cube in a saucepan, cover with cold water and then place over high heat. Bring to the boil, then reduce the heat to medium. Simmer, stirring occasionally, for 10–12 minutes until the potato is tender. Drain, return to the pan and mash well. Season.

Meanwhile, heat a large chargrill pan over medium–high heat. Add the barramundi and chargrill for 4 minutes on one side. Carefully turn the fish and add the asparagus to the chargrill. Chargrill for 4 minutes, turning the asparagus occasionally, until the fish is just cooked and golden.

Serve the mash, barramundi and asparagus with the creamy lemon sauce and parsley, if using.

Family additions Serve with mashed potatoes or garlic bread.

 Calorie boosters

Serve with ½ cup mashed potatoes (with a dash of full-cream milk and butter).	119 cals

The recipes

Dinner

Tantalising Thai yellow fish curry

Serves 4 | Prep 15 minutes | Cook 10 minutes | Cals per serve 219

It doesn't get much better than finishing the day with this curry, imagining yourself on a relaxing beach holiday in Phuket. You can easily swap out the fish for tofu or chickpeas for a veggie alternative, and serve with konjac, cauliflower or jasmine rice.

¼ cup (55 g) Thai yellow curry paste
1 ½ cups (375 ml) **Herbaceous vegetable broth** (page 115)
⅓ cup (80 ml) light coconut cream
500 g peeled, seeded and thinly sliced butternut pumpkin
500 g skinless boneless thick white fish fillets, cut into 3 cm pieces
1 red capsicum, cut into 3 cm pieces
300 g sugar snap peas, trimmed
lime halves, to serve (optional)
½ cup coriander leaves
½ cup small basil leaves

Heat the curry paste in a large, deep non-stick frying pan over medium–high heat. Cook, stirring, for 1 minute or until fragrant. Stir in the Herbaceous vegetable broth and coconut cream and bring just to the boil.

Reduce the heat to medium–low and add the pumpkin and fish. Simmer gently, stirring carefully and occasionally, for 5 minutes.

Add the capsicum and sugar snaps and cook, partially covered and untouched, for 3–4 minutes until the fish and vegetables are just cooked. Remove from the heat and leave the pan covered for 2 minutes.

Serve in bowls with lime halves, if using, sprinkled with coriander and basil.

Family additions Serve with jasmine rice and sprinkle with bean sprouts and chopped toasted peanuts.

Calorie boosters

Serve with konjac rice or	10 cals
½ cup cooked jasmine rice.	120 cals

The recipes

Dinner

Roast salmon with veggie fries and SFD terrific tartare sauce

Serves 4 Prep 15 minutes Cook 20 minutes Cals per serve 232

Let us list why we love salmon oh so much … this fabulous fish includes protective antioxidants, high-quality protein, vitamins, and minerals, and of course a whole lot of omega-3 fatty acids. So sofishticated.

300 g sweet potato, cut into thick matchsticks
4 zucchini, cut into thick matchsticks
2 carrots, cut into batons
400 g baby green beans, trimmed (optional)
4 x 120 g skinless boneless salmon fillets
2 tablespoons dill leaves
olive oil cooking spray
1 lemon, cut into wedges
mixed salad leaves, to serve

SFD tartare sauce
¾ cup **Creamy dollop** (page 112)
2 teaspoons baby capers, finely chopped
2 sweet gherkins, finely chopped
2 tablespoons finely chopped flat-leaf parsley

Preheat the oven to 220°C (200°C fan-forced). Line a large baking tray with non-stick baking paper.

Make the SFD tartare sauce by stirring together all the ingredients in a small bowl. Season and refrigerate until required.

Place the sweet potato, zucchini, carrot, beans (if using), salmon and dill in a large bowl. Season and lightly spray with oil. Toss gently to coat well. Spread out evenly over the baking tray, making sure the salmon fillets are sitting flat and not covered by the vegetables.

Roast for 15–18 minutes, turning the salmon once, until the veggie fries are crispy and the salmon is cooked to your liking. Arrange on serving plates and serve with SFD tartare sauce, lemon wedges and mixed salad leaves.

Note

- You can make the SFD tartare sauce up to 12 hours in advance and store in an airtight container in the fridge (the parsley will discolour slightly).

Family additions Increase the amounts of sweet potato and salmon per serve.

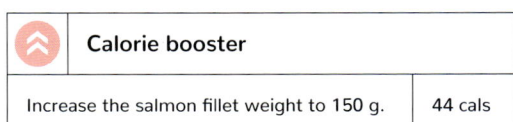

	Calorie booster	
	Increase the salmon fillet weight to 150 g.	44 cals

The 3-Day Diet

Dinner

Tuna and veggie macaroni bake

Serves 4 | Prep 15 minutes | Cook 30 minutes | Cals per serve 316

Holy macaroni! Wouldn't you love a baked mac, with none of the bad stuff and plenty of the great stuff? We've got you covered! Trick the kiddies (or yourself) into a veggie-filled, healthy and equally delectable macaroni bake, for a simple weeknight throw together.

olive oil cooking spray
4 zucchini, chopped into 2 cm pieces
2 celery stalks, chopped into 2 cm pieces
400 g peeled and seeded Kent pumpkin, chopped into 2 cm pieces
½ cup **Basic veggie paste** (page 113)
¾ cup (100 g) macaroni
425 g tuna in springwater, drained and flaked
50 g bocconcini, coarsely grated
¼ cup panko breadcrumbs
½ teaspoon dried mixed herbs

Preheat the oven to 200°C (180°C fan-forced). Lightly spray a deep 28 x 20 cm baking dish with oil.

Add the zucchini, celery, pumpkin and Basic veggie paste to the dish, stirring to combine and coat well. Season. Bake for 15 minutes, or until starting to soften and golden.

Meanwhile, cook the macaroni in boiling water for 3 minutes only. Drain and refresh under cold running water. Drain well.

Carefully add the macaroni and tuna to the baking dish, stirring together to combine and coat well. Sprinkle with the bocconcini, then the combined panko and herbs. Season, then lightly spray the top with oil.

Bake for 12–15 minutes or until the cheese softens and the top is golden and crisp. Leave to rest in the dish for 5 minutes before serving.

Note
- You need to chop all the veggies to roughly the same size so they cook in the same timeframe.

Family additions Drizzle with basil pesto and serve with steamed green beans and peas.

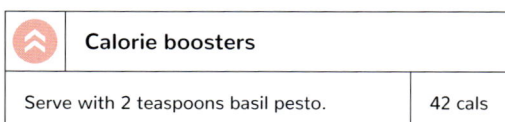

Calorie boosters	
Serve with 2 teaspoons basil pesto.	42 cals

Dinner

Fancy filo-topped salmon pie

Serves 4   **Prep** 15 minutes   **Cook** 20 minutes   **Cals per serve** 258

Pie on a fast day? That's a big YES! We only have 'pies' for this stunner of a meal that the whole family can chow down on. It also freezes wonderfully so you can enjoy it at a later date when you are running low on time but want a big flavour hit (minus the calories).

600 g skinless boneless salmon fillets, chopped into 2 cm pieces
2 spring onions, sliced
2 carrots, finely chopped
2 celery stalks, finely chopped
1½ cups (375 ml) **Vegelicious tomato sauce** (page 114)
olive oil cooking spray
4 sheets filo pastry
mixed salad leaves, to serve

Preheat the oven to 180°C (160°C fan-forced). Combine the salmon, onion, carrot, celery and Vegelicious tomato sauce in a bowl. Season and then transfer to a deep 28 x 20 cm baking dish.

Lightly spray each filo sheet with oil, then carefully and loosely scrunch them up. Arrange on top of the salmon mixture. Bake for 15–18 minutes until the salmon is cooked and the pastry is golden and crisp.

Take straight to the table and serve with mixed salad leaves.

Family additions Serve with any mashed potato.

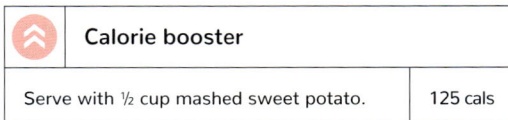

	Calorie booster
Serve with ½ cup mashed sweet potato.	125 cals

Dinner

Sesame beef and radish salad

Serves 4 | Prep 15 minutes | Cook 15 minutes | Cals per serve 236

Fun and funky new salad combos are our jam! Full of filling healthy fats thanks to our favourite, avo, along with colourful and vitamin-rich vegetables and protein-rich beef strips ... just typing this out, our mouths are beginning to salivate a little ... alright we'd better stop!

2 teaspoons sesame seeds
400 g beef stir-fry strips
1 onion, cut into thin strips

Radish salad
2 bunches baby red radishes, thinly sliced
2 carrots, cut into matchsticks
1 avocado, sliced
2 tablespoons **Tamari–ginger drizzle** (page 112)
100 g baby spinach leaves

Combine the sesame seeds, beef and onion in a bowl and season. Preheat a large chargrill pan over high heat.

Chargrill the beef mixture in three separate batches, for 4–5 minutes each batch, turning occasionally until cooked and golden. Transfer to a bowl and season.

Make the radish salad by combining the ingredients in a bowl. Season, stir in the beef mixture and arrange on serving plates. Serve warm.

Family additions Add cooked udon noodles to the salad mixture or serve with cooked rice.

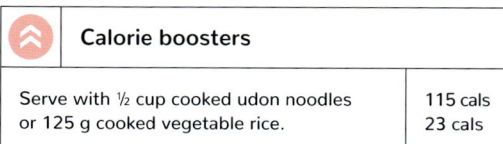

Calorie boosters	
Serve with ½ cup cooked udon noodles	115 cals
or 125 g cooked vegetable rice.	23 cals

Dinner

Hearty but healthy turkey nachos

Serves 4 **Prep** 15 minutes **Cook** 4 hours **Cals per serve** 191

Healthy Mexican options are really having their moment right now. Turkey is one of the best lean, low-calorie protein options out there, coming in at just under **100** calories per serve. It is even better mixed in with salsa and our fabulous home-made SFD dried spice mix!

400 g turkey breast strips
300 g jar chunky tomato salsa
2 tablespoons **Basic dried spice blend** (page 113)
1 avocado, thinly sliced
2 spring onions, thinly sliced
1 baby cos, leaves separated
2 limes, cut into wedges
coriander leaves, to serve (optional)

Preheat a slow cooker to High. Add the turkey, salsa, Basic dried spice blend and ½ cup (125 ml) water. Cover and slow cook for 4 hours. Shred the meat into a bowl, then season and stir to combine.

Divide the turkey mixture among serving bowls, and top with avocado and spring onion. Serve with lettuce leaves for scooping, and lime wedges.

Family additions Serve on corn chips with Greek yoghurt.

	Calorie booster	
	Serve with 1 tablespoon non-fat plain Greek yoghurt.	54 cals

The 3-Day Diet

Dinner

Chargrilled pork and grape salad

Serves 4 | Prep 20 minutes | Cook 15 minutes | Cals per serve 348

Grapes are the perfect sweet addition to this wholesome knockout salad. Best of all, most of the work has been done for you, as store-bought kale slaw salad mix eliminates extra chopping!

300 g lean pork loin fillet, thinly sliced
400 g yellow squash, sliced
1 red onion, thinly sliced
3 teaspoons smoked paprika
olive oil cooking spray
350 g packet kale slaw salad mix
100 g seedless grapes, sliced
200 g crunchy sprouts combo
1 bunch baby red radishes, thinly sliced

Preheat a large chargrill pan over medium–high heat. Combine the pork, squash, onion and smoked paprika in a bowl. Season, then spray with oil. Toss to combine and coat well.

Chargrill the pork mixture in two separate batches, for 5–6 minutes each batch, turning occasionally, until cooked and golden. Transfer to a bowl.

Toss together the kale slaw salad mix (including its dressing sachet), grapes, sprouts and radish. Arrange on serving plates, top with the pork mixture and serve warm.

Family additions Add steamed sweet potato and sourdough croutons.

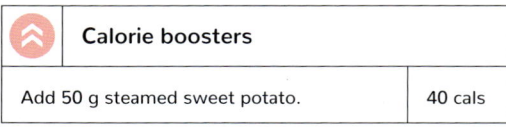

Calorie boosters	
Add 50 g steamed sweet potato.	40 cals

Dinner

Slow-cooker lamb and sweet potato casserole

Serves 4   **Prep** 15 minutes   **Cook** 4 hours   **Cals per serve** 293

Coming home to a wholesome, warm and wintery meal is one of life's simple joys. Made with two of our staples, this ultimate hearty casserole can be ready for you when you arrive home, exhausted after a long day.

400 g lamb backstrap, chopped
2 cups (500 ml) **Vegelicious tomato sauce** (page 114)
2 tablespoons **Basic dried spice blend** (page 113)
400 g peeled and chopped sweet potato
50 g baby spinach leaves
2 x 250 g packets cauliflower and broccoli rice, heated as per packet instructions

Preheat a slow cooker to High. Add the lamb, Vegelicious tomato sauce, Basic dried spice blend and sweet potato, cover and cook for 4 hours.

Add the spinach to the slow cooker. Cover and cook for 15 minutes, or until wilted. Season and stir well.

Spoon the vegetable rice into bowls and top with the lamb mixture to serve.

Note

- Don't have a slow cooker? Add the lamb, Vegelicious tomato sauce, Basic dried spice blend and sweet potato to a heavy-based saucepan over medium–low heat. Simmer gently for 2 hours, stirring occasionally, then add the spinach and stir until wilted.

Family additions Replace the vegetable rice with long-grain rice or mashed potato.

Calorie booster	
Add an extra 125 g cooked vegetable rice (e.g. cauliflower).	23 cals

Dinner

Tip-top tamari pork stir-fry

Serves 4   **Prep** 15 minutes   **Cook** 15 minutes   **Cals per serve** 396

The perfect 'fake-away' for the 'I can't be bothered' Friday-night dinner. You've got to love an Asian-fusion dish to transport our tastebuds to tropical places far away!

2 tablespoons **Tamari–ginger drizzle** (page 112)
300 g lean pork loin fillet, cut into thin strips
olive oil cooking spray
2 tablespoons chopped raw cashews
400 g sugar snap peas, trimmed
400 g snow peas, trimmed
1 yellow capsicum, cut into strips
2 cups (370 g) cooked jasmine rice, to serve
1 lime, cut into wedges
spring onion, shredded, to serve (optional)

Combine the Tamari–ginger drizzle and pork in a bowl. Season.

Heat a large non-stick wok over high heat. Spray with oil. Stir-fry the pork in 3 batches, for 3–4 minutes each batch, until just cooked and golden.

Return all the pork to the wok over high heat. Add the cashews and vegetables and stir-fry for 2 minutes, or until the vegetables are just tender.

Serve the pork stir-fry over jasmine rice, with lime wedges, then sprinkle with spring onion, if using.

Note
- You can leave the pork mixture to marinate for up to 24 hours in step 1; store in an airtight container in the fridge.

Family additions Serve with extra jasmine rice and add toasted cashews.

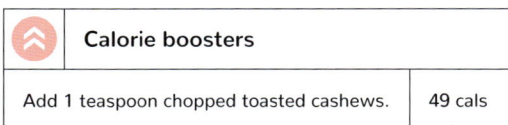

Calorie boosters	
Add 1 teaspoon chopped toasted cashews.	49 cals

The recipes

Dinner

Peppered beef and strawberry salad

 Serves 4

 Prep 15 minutes + 5 minutes resting

 Cook 10 minutes

 Cals per serve 184

This salad is the perfect 'everyone bring a plate to the BBQ' option! Easy to share or whip up on a weeknight, there is something about adding berries to a salad for that extra pizzazz.

4 x 120 g beef fillet steaks
1 tablespoon cracked black pepper
2 teaspoons cumin seeds
olive oil cooking spray

Strawberry salad
300 g baby leaf salad mix
250 g small strawberries, halved
250 g baby cucumbers, sliced
⅓ cup (80 ml) **Virtually no-cal-gal dressing** (page 112)

Coat the steaks evenly on both sides with the combined pepper and cumin seeds. Spray with oil.

Preheat a large non-stick frying pan over medium–high heat. Pan-fry the steaks for 4 minutes each side for medium, or until cooked to your liking. Transfer to a wooden board and leave to rest for 5 minutes before slicing.

Meanwhile, make the strawberry salad by combining the ingredients in a bowl. Season.

Arrange the Strawberry salad and sliced steak on plates to serve.

Family additions Increase the beef per serve, add mixed antipasto vegetables and serve with wholemeal flatbreads.

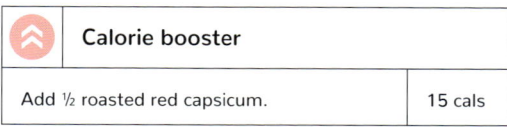

The 3-Day Diet

Dinner

Herb-crumbed lamb cutlets and slaw

Serves 4 | Prep 20 minutes + 15 minutes chilling | Cook 20 minutes | Cals per serve 216

Lamb cutlets are such an easy dinner staple, but crumbing them with panko breadcrumbs and herbs adds loads of flavour and fanciness that we just all could use sometimes.

1 egg white, whisked
1 tablespoon chopped thyme leaves
1 tablespoon chopped rosemary leaves
2 tablespoons finely chopped chives
¼ cup panko breadcrumbs
1 tablespoon plain flour
12 small lean French-trimmed lamb cutlets, seasoned
200 g packet classic coleslaw mix
¼ cup (60 ml) **Creamy dollop** (page 112)
50 g baby rocket leaves
olive oil cooking spray
1 lemon, cut into wedges

Place the egg white in a large shallow bowl, season and whisk with 1 tablespoon water. Combine the herbs and panko in a separate shallow bowl and season. Dust the lamb cutlets lightly with flour on both sides, shaking off the excess. Lightly dip each cutlet into the egg white, then the panko. Put on a plate, cover and chill for 15 minutes.

Meanwhile, combine the coleslaw and Creamy dollop in a bowl. Season and toss gently with the rocket. Chill until required.

Heat a large non-stick frying pan over medium–high heat and spray with oil. Cook the lamb cutlets in two batches for 7–8 minutes each batch, turning only once, until cooked and golden.

Serve the coleslaw and lamb cutlets with the lemon wedges.

Family additions Serve with baked potato wedges.

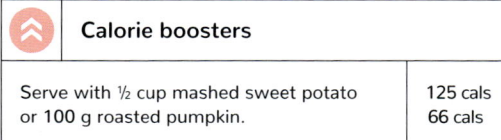

Calorie boosters	
Serve with ½ cup mashed sweet potato or 100 g roasted pumpkin.	125 cals 66 cals

Dinner

Mongolian beef with veggie noodles

Serves 4   **Prep** 15 minutes   **Cook** 15 minutes   **Cals per serve** 169

We love whipping up new ideas that allow us to enjoy our beloved takeaway options, and this tasty take on a Chinese favourite is no exception. Using veggie noodles beefs up your meal (see what we did there?), boosts your veggie intake and lowers those cals.

400 g beef stir-fry strips
2 tablespoons **Tamari–ginger drizzle** (page 112)
1 tablespoon hoisin sauce
1 green capsicum, cut into strips
1 red capsicum, cut into strips
olive oil cooking spray
4 spring onions, cut into 3 cm lengths
500 g fresh zucchini and carrot noodles

Combine the beef, Tamari–ginger drizzle, hoisin and capsicum in a bowl and spray with oil. Heat a large non-stick wok over high heat.

Stir-fry the beef mixture in four separate batches, for 3 minutes each batch, or until cooked and golden.

Return all the mixture to the wok, add the spring onion, noodles and 2 tablespoons water and stir-fry for 30 seconds to combine. Serve in bowls.

Family additions Serve with hokkien noodles and extra beef.

 Calorie booster

Serve with ½ cup cooked hokkien noodles.	110 cals

Dinner

Pumpkin–chickpea patties with fab feta yoghurt

Serves 4 | Prep 25 minutes + 20 minutes chilling | Cook 25 minutes | Cals per serve 292 | Vegetarian

Here's our vegetarian take for a family-favourite burger night.

300 g peeled, seeded and diced butternut pumpkin
400 g can chickpeas, rinsed well
2 tablespoons panko breadcrumbs
1 egg white, whisked
1 tablespoon **Basic dried spice blend** (page 113)
½ cup **Creamy dollop** (page 112)
50 g Danish feta, crumbled
2 tablespoons finely chopped basil
olive oil cooking spray
400 g baby green beans, trimmed
4 zucchini, cut into matchsticks
1 lemon, cut into wedges

Steam the pumpkin over boiling water for 8–10 minutes or until almost tender. Drain well, transfer to a bowl and mash. Add the chickpeas and mash. Add the panko, egg white and Basic dried spice blend. Season and stir together until well combined.

Shape ¼ cup measures of the mixture into eight round patties, each around 6 cm wide. Place on a baking paper-lined tray, cover and refrigerate for 20 minutes to set firm (this is important so they hold their shape when turned during cooking).

Meanwhile, combine the Creamy dollop, feta and basil in a bowl and chill until required.

Preheat a large non-stick frying pan over medium–high heat. Spray with oil. Cook the patties for 3–4 minutes on each side until cooked and golden.

Steam the beans and zucchini together over boiling water for 3–4 minutes until just tender. Arrange on plates and top with the patties. Spoon the feta yoghurt over the top and serve with lemon wedges.

Notes
- You can also microwave the pumpkin, covered, on High for 3 minutes.
- If you have time, make the patties a day in advance and keep covered in the fridge; the longer they chill, the firmer they become, which makes cooking easier.

Family additions Serve the patties inside a soft, seeded burger bun.

Calorie boosters	
Serve the patties inside a burger thin (like a sandwich thin but round).	84 cals

Dinner

Green machine cannellini stew

Serves	Prep	Cook	Cals per serve	Vegan
4	15 minutes	15 minutes	210	

Whip out that vegetable broth and combine it with veggies and cannellini beans, and you've got yourself this hearty green machine of a stew. This will absolutely become one of your satisfying fast-day fillers, we just know it. Get your green on!

4 cups (1 litre) **Herbaceous vegetable broth** (page 115)
2 zucchini, chopped
300 g baby green beans, trimmed
4 yellow squash, sliced
2 baby fennel, chopped
400 g can cannellini beans, rinsed well
¼ cup (55 g) risoni
2 spring onions, thinly sliced
2 tablespoons basil pesto

Stir together the Herbaceous vegetable broth, vegetables, beans, risoni and spring onion in a large saucepan over medium–high heat. Bring to a rapid simmer, stirring, then reduce to medium heat. Simmer, partially covered and stirring occasionally, for 10–12 minutes until the vegetables and risoni are cooked. Season.

Spoon into serving bowls and serve with basil pesto.

Family additions Increase the cannellini beans, risoni and basil pesto per serve.

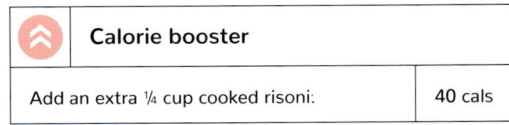

Calorie booster	
Add an extra ¼ cup cooked risoni.	40 cals

Dinner

Friday night flatbread pizzas

Serves	Prep	Cook	Cals per serve	Vegetarian
4	15 minutes	25 minutes	339	

Pizza. Must we say more? We love pizza, and the fact it is always a recommended and well-loved 3-day diet meal staple makes us some pretty happy campers. You'll never need to dial Domino's again!

4 large wholemeal flatbreads
1 small red onion, thinly sliced
4 pieces roasted capsicum, cut into thin strips
4 pieces roasted eggplant, cut into thin strips
250 g baby tomatoes, halved
200 g Danish feta, crumbled
¼ cup (60 ml) **Thyme-ly mustard dressing** (page 112)
mixed salad leaves, to serve
basil leaves, to serve (optional)

Preheat the oven to 200°C (180°C fan-forced).

Sprinkle each flatbread with the onion, capsicum, eggplant, tomato and feta. Bake two flatbreads at a time, directly on the oven shelf, for 10–12 minutes until the bases are crisp and the tops golden.

Transfer to serving plates and drizzle with the Thyme-ly mustard dressing. Serve with mixed salad leaves and basil, if using.

Family additions Sprinkle grated mozzarella over the pizzas before baking.

 Calorie boosters

Serve sprinkled with 1 teaspoon chopped toasted pecans.	47 cals

Dinner

Broccoli and feta frittata with crouton topping

Serves 4   **Prep** 15 minutes + 5 minutes resting   **Cook** 30 minutes   **Cals per serve** 380   **Vegetarian**

Looking for a fun and fresh take on the classic frittata? You can't go wrong with this scrummy one, featuring vibrant greens and a crunchy crouton finish.

olive oil cooking spray
8 eggs, whisked
500 g small broccoli florets
200 g green beans, sliced
¼ cup **Basic spice paste** (page 113)
100 g Danish feta, crumbled
4 slices wholegrain bread, diced into 1 cm cubes
mixed salad leaves, to serve

Preheat the oven to 180°C (160°C fan-forced). Lightly spray a deep 28 x 20 cm baking dish with oil.

Place the eggs in a large bowl with ¼ cup (60 ml) water. Season and whisk together. Stir in the broccoli, beans, Basic spice paste and feta. Pour into the dish and level the surface.

Sprinkle the top with bread cubes. Season, then lightly spray with oil. Bake for 25–30 minutes or until set and golden.

Leave to rest in the dish for 5 minutes, then serve with mixed salad leaves.

Family additions Serve with extra Danish feta, garlic bread or steamed mixed vegetables.

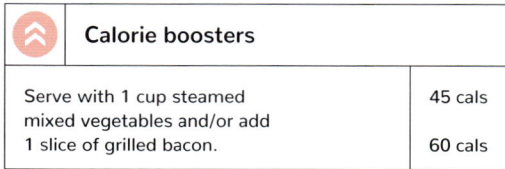

	Calorie boosters	
	Serve with 1 cup steamed mixed vegetables and/or add	45 cals
	1 slice of grilled bacon.	60 cals

Dinner

Mushroom and bean goulash soup

 Serves 4
 Prep 15 minutes
 Cook 15 minutes
 Cals per serve 277
 Vegetarian

Sick of the same old veggie soup? Pack a nutritional punch with this marvellous mushroom and black bean soup. Perfect on its own for a fast-day filler or poured over some delicious pasta or zoodles (zucchini noodles) for an Italian twist.

olive oil cooking spray
300 g button mushrooms, halved
3 teaspoons sweet paprika
400 g can black beans, rinsed well
4 cups (1 litre) **Vegelicious tomato sauce** (page 114)
200 g baby potatoes, unpeeled, quartered
½ cup chopped flat-leaf parsley
¼ cup non-fat plain Greek yoghurt

Heat a large saucepan over medium–high heat. Spray with oil. Add the mushroom and paprika and cook, stirring, for 3 minutes or until starting to soften.

Add the beans, Vegelicious tomato sauce, potato and 1 cup (250 ml) water. Bring to the boil, stirring, then reduce the heat to medium–low. Simmer for 10–12 minutes until the potato is just tender. Remove from the heat and season.

Stir in the parsley and spoon into bowls. Served topped with yoghurt.

Family additions Serve over cooked pasta.

⌃	Calorie booster	
	Serve with a toasted wholemeal sandwich thin.	99 cals

Dinner

Mexican bean and roast pumpkin salad

Serves 4 | Prep 20 minutes + 5 minutes cooling | Cook 20 minutes | Cals per serve 318 | Vegan

This tasty Mexican-inspired vegan salad is filled to the brim with spiced beans, radiant roast pumpkin and veggies galore!

1 red onion, very thinly sliced
2 tablespoons red wine vinegar
600 g peeled and seeded Kent pumpkin, cut into 5 mm-thick slices
1 tablespoon **Basic dried spice blend** (page 113)
olive oil cooking spray
2 x 400 g cans red kidney beans, rinsed well
2 celery stalks, thinly sliced
1 red capsicum, thinly sliced
1 avocado, sliced
3 baby cos lettuces, leaves separated
lime halves and coriander leaves, to serve (optional)

Preheat the oven to 200°C (180°C fan-forced). Line a large baking tray with non-stick baking paper.

Combine the onion and vinegar in a small bowl. Season, then stir well. Set aside, stirring occasionally, until softened.

Meanwhile, place the pumpkin on the baking tray, sprinkle on both sides with the Basic dried spice blend, then lightly spray with oil. Bake for 18–20 minutes until cooked and dark golden. Transfer to a large bowl and leave to cool for 5 minutes.

Add the onion mixture to the bowl with the pumpkin. Add the kidney beans, celery, capsicum, avocado and lettuce and toss gently to combine. Season and serve warm with lime halves and coriander, if using.

Family additions Serve with toasted tortillas and plain coconut yoghurt.

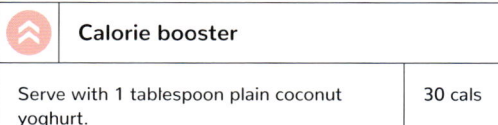

	Calorie booster	
	Serve with 1 tablespoon plain coconut yoghurt.	30 cals

Dinner

Mushroom kebabs and quinoa tabbouli

Serves 4 | Prep 25 minutes | Cook 25 minutes | Cals per serve (3 skewers) 176 | Vegan

Create the perfect Middle Eastern feast at home with these vegan kebabs that are super-duper good for you.

400 g button mushrooms
400 g Swiss brown mushrooms
200 g fresh shiitake mushrooms, halved
1 onion, cut into 2 cm pieces (optional)
3 teaspoons smoked paprika
olive oil cooking spray
½ cup (125 ml) Creamy dollop (page 112)
lemon wedges, to serve (optional)

Quinoa tabbouli
½ cup (100 g) quinoa
1 small red onion, finely chopped
2 Lebanese cucumbers, finely chopped
1 green capsicum, finely chopped
1 cup chopped flat-leaf parsley
¼ cup finely chopped mint
¼ cup finely chopped coriander

To make the quinoa tabbouli, cook the quinoa in a saucepan of boiling water for 13–15 minutes until cooked. Drain, refresh under cold running water, then drain well. Place in a bowl, season and toss with the remaining ingredients. Chill until required.

Combine the mushrooms, onion (if using) and smoked paprika in a bowl. Season, spray with oil and toss to coat well. Thread evenly onto 12 metal skewers, alternating mushrooms and onions (if using). Preheat a large chargrill pan over high heat.

Chargrill the skewers in two separate batches, turning occasionally, for 5 minutes each batch, or until just cooked and golden.

Spoon the tabbouli onto plates and serve with the mushroom skewers, Creamy dollop and lemon wedges, if using.

Family additions Serve with pita bread, hummus and pickled vegetables.

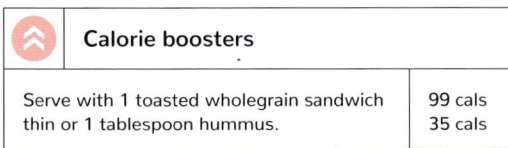

Calorie boosters	
Serve with 1 toasted wholegrain sandwich thin or 1 tablespoon hummus.	99 cals 35 cals

Dinner

Mexican sweet potato boats

Serves
4

Prep
15 minutes +
10 minutes resting

Cook
45 minutes

Cals per serve
292

Vegan

This awesome mix of protein-rich beans and smart carbs, thanks to the sweet potato, will definitely float your boat.

4 x 150 g sweet potatoes, halved lengthways
400 g four-bean mix, rinsed well
125 g can sweetcorn, rinsed well
300 g jar chunky tomato salsa
1 red capsicum, finely chopped
2 tablespoons finely chopped coriander
1 avocado, diced

Preheat the oven to 200°C (180°C fan-forced). Line a large baking tray with non-stick baking paper. Put the sweet potato on the tray and cover loosely with a tent of foil.

Bake for 40–45 minutes until just tender. Leave on the tray, covered with foil, for 10 minutes.

Meanwhile, combine the beans with the remaining ingredients in a bowl. Season.

Arrange two sweet potato halves on each plate and spoon the bean mixture over the top to serve.

Family additions Use larger sweet potatoes and add more beans. Serve with plain coconut yoghurt and extra avocado.

Calorie boosters	
Use larger 200 g sweet potatoes.	30 cals

Dinner

Tasty tempeh tacos

 Serves 4
 Prep 20 minutes
 Cook 10 minutes
 Cals per serve 217
 Vegan

Not only does tempeh provide a punch of protein, it is also full of essential vitamins, plus plenty of prebiotics, which helps digestive health. Who would've thought this awesome plant-based source could provide so much nutty goodness?

olive oil cooking spray
300 g tempeh, finely chopped
1 red onion, finely chopped
2 zucchini, finely chopped
1 green capsicum, finely chopped
2 tablespoons **Basic dried spice blend** (page 113)
1 small iceberg lettuce, leaves separated into cups
300 g jar tomato salsa
2 Lebanese cucumbers, finely chopped

Heat a large non-stick frying pan over medium–high heat and spray with oil. Add the tempeh, onion, zucchini, capsicum and Basic dried spice blend, then lightly spray with more oil. Cook, stirring, for 6–7 minutes until the vegetables are soft and golden.

Spoon the tempeh mixture into the iceberg cups to serve. Spoon the salsa over the top, followed by the cucumber.

Family additions Serve the tempeh mixture in heated taco shells, and top with mashed avocado and vegan sour cream.

 Calorie booster

Add 125 g konjac rice to the tempeh mixture or top with 25 g chopped avocado.	10 cals 40 cals

The 3-Day Diet

Dinner

Cauli-freddo with crispy kale

Serves
4

Prep
25 minutes

Cook
15 minutes

Cals per serve
114

Vegan

When you think of cauliflower, do you immediately think of a gorgeous creamy pasta sauce? No? Get ready to have your mind blown! This gorgeous, velvety vegan sauce poured over crunchy veggie noodles is sure to satisfy those persistent pasta cravings without the calories.

4 kale leaves, stems discarded, leaves torn into 3 cm pieces
olive oil spray
2 teaspoons **Basic dried spice blend** (page 113)
400 g cauliflower florets, chopped
½ cup (125 ml) **Herbaceous vegetable broth** (page 115)
40 g cashew cheese
500 g fresh zucchini and carrot noodles
½ cup small basil leaves
2 tablespoons toasted pine nuts

Preheat the oven to 180°C (160°C fan-forced). Line a large baking tray with non-stick baking paper. Lay the kale in a single layer on the tray, spray very lightly with oil, then sprinkle with the Basic dried spice blend. Bake for 12–15 minutes until golden crisp. Cool the kale on the tray.

Meanwhile, place the cauliflower and Herbaceous vegetable broth in a large saucepan over high heat. Bring to the boil and cook, stirring occasionally, for 6–8 minutes until the cauliflower is tender and almost all of the broth has evaporated. Cool slightly.

Add the cashew cheese to the cauliflower mixture and blend using a hand-held blender until completely smooth, adding a very small amount of water to loosen if needed – it should have the consistency of thick custard. Transfer to a large bowl.

Add the vegetable noodles to the bowl. Season and toss to coat well. Serve in bowls, topped with the crispy kale and basil leaves, and sprinkled with pine nuts.

Family additions Serve with cooked spaghetti, cooked mushrooms and basil pesto.

Calorie booster	
Add 100 g cooked mushrooms or drizzle with 2 teaspoons basil pesto.	28 cals 40 cals

Dinner

Lentil-as-anything bolognese

Serves 4   **Prep** 15 minutes   **Cook** 15 minutes   **Cals per serve** 370   **Vegan**

Bolognese is a family favourite in almost every household. Want to make it meat-free and less calorie dense? Look no further! Made with lentils, our very own Vegelicious tomato sauce and served on veggie noodles, it is a complete combo of goodness.

4 cups (1 litre) **Vegelicious tomato sauce** (page 114)
2 x 400 g cans brown lentils, rinsed well
1 bunch silverbeet, white stalks discarded, leaves shredded
¾ cup (100 g) pulse pasta
500 g packets fresh zucchini and carrot noodles
½ cup basil leaves

Stir the Vegelicious tomato sauce and lentils in a large saucepan over medium heat until the mixture comes to a rapid simmer. Reduce the heat to medium–low. Simmer gently for 10 minutes.

Add the silverbeet to the pan in batches, stirring so it wilts a little before adding the next batch. Simmer for 2–3 minutes until all the silverbeet has wilted and the sauce has thickened slightly.

Cook the pasta as per the packet instructions. Drain.

Divide the pasta and noodles among serving bowls and top with the lentil mixture. Serve sprinkled with basil leaves.

Family additions Serve with cooked spaghetti, crumbled cashew cheese, toasted pine nuts and vegan garlic bread.

 Calorie boosters

Serve with ½ cup cooked spaghetti or add an extra 100 g brown lentils.	110 cals 116 cals

Dinner

Roast cauli, tofu and orange salad

Serves 4 | Prep 20 minutes | Cook 20 minutes | Cals per serve 262 | Vegan

We simply adore a sweet and salty mix. And by golly, we think we've mastered it here. For a delicious vegan protein hit, it's hard to go past tofu, and when paired with golden roasted cauliflower and the sweet citrus of oranges, good luck trying to pass this one up!

300 g firm tofu, cut into 1 cm cubes
600 g cauliflower florets
400 g brussels sprouts, halved
olive oil cooking spray
⅓ cup (80 ml) **Tamari–ginger drizzle** (page 112)
2 small naval oranges, peel and white pith removed, sliced into thin rounds
300 g mixed baby leaf salad

Preheat the oven to 200°C (180°C fan-forced). Line a large baking tray with non-stick baking paper. Arrange the tofu, cauliflower and sprouts on the tray, lightly spray with oil and season.

Bake for 15–18 minutes until cooked and golden crisp. Transfer to a large bowl, add the Tamari–ginger drizzle and toss to coat well. Leave to cool for 3 minutes.

Add the orange slices and salad mix to the bowl and toss gently. Serve warm.

Family additions Add chopped sweet potato to the baking tray; serve with crunchy fried noodles and chopped avocado tossed through the salad.

 Calorie booster

| Add 25 g chopped avocado or | 40 cals |
| 2 teaspoons chopped roasted walnuts. | 90 cals |

100 CALORIE

SNACKS & DRINKS

Snacks & Drinks

Roast pumpkin dip

Serves	Prep	Cook	Cals per serve	Vegan
4	15 minutes	15 minutes	361	

Dips are one of our favourite snacks to whip up at home to avoid the 'nasties' you so often find in store-bought brands. Serve this with a variety of gorgeous crunchy veg and you are good to go. Dip in.

500 g peeled, seeded butternut pumpkin, diced into 2 cm cubes
1 tablespoon cumin seeds
olive oil cooking spray
2 tablespoons lemon juice
1 bunch baby red radishes, halved lengthways
1 baby cos, leaves separated
1 bunch baby carrots, peeled
250 g baby cucumbers, halved lengthways (optional)

Preheat the oven to 200°C (180°C fan-forced). Line a large baking tray with non-stick baking paper. Spread the pumpkin over the tray, sprinkle with the cumin, then season and spray with oil.

Bake for 20 minutes, or until cooked and golden. Cool on the tray for 3 minutes, then transfer to a food processor.

Add the lemon juice and process until smooth. Transfer to a bowl and serve warm with the radish, cos leaves, carrot and cucumber (if using) for dipping.

Family additions Serve on a tasting plate with toasted sliced baguette and cheeses of choice.

Calorie boosters

Serve with 10 small seeded crackers,	120 cals
50 g pita bread or	153 cals
10 rice crackers.	72 cals

Snacks & Drinks

Divine dates with lime ricotta

Serves 4 | Prep 15 minutes | Cals per serve 94 | Vegetarian

There is no doubt that a sweet snack is sometimes a necessity. And we don't think you can beat these loaded lime ricotta dates. You can elevate the deliciousness by sprinkling over a little grated dark chocolate too.

- 2 tablespoons fresh ricotta
- 1 tablespoon lime juice
- 2 teaspoons finely grated lime zest
- 4 large fresh medjool dates, split lengthways and pitted

Mix together the ricotta, lime juice and 1 teaspoon of the zest. Spoon into the date halves. Serve sprinkled with the remaining lime zest.

Family additions Increase to 3 date halves per person and sprinkle generously with grated chocolate.

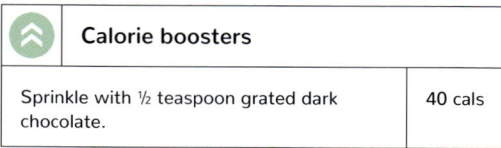

Calorie boosters	
Sprinkle with ½ teaspoon grated dark chocolate.	40 cals

Snacks & Drinks

Zucchini salsa melts

Serves	Prep	Cook	Cals per serve	Vegetarian
4	15 minutes	5 minutes	56	

Ditch those savoury cravings with this fabulous low-carb snack with plenty of fantastic flavour. These melts give off a 'mini pizza' vibe. Make them even more pizza-esque by popping on some lean ham to boost the calories (and the deliciousness).

2 large zucchini, halved lengthways
½ cup tomato salsa
25 g sliced reduced-fat Swiss cheese

Preheat an oven grill to high. Using a teaspoon, scrape out the seeds from the centre of the zucchini halves. Cut into 4 cm lengths, then place on a baking tray. Spoon salsa into the cavities and top with cheese.

Place under the grill for 1–2 minutes until the cheese has melted and is light golden. Serve warm.

Family additions Add shaved ham and more cheese.

Calorie booster

Add an extra 25 g reduced-fat Swiss cheese.	84 cals

Mango fro-yo pops

Makes 6 ice pops | Prep 15 minutes | Freezing 4 hours | Cals per serve 64 | Vegan

Say hello to our favourite new sweet delight. Not only are these goodies vegan, they are also nutrient-dense, full of healthy fats thanks to the creamy coconut yoghurt, and packed with immunity-boosting properties! Hot tip: dip your frozen pop into melted dark chocolate.

1 cup (250 g) natural coconut yoghurt
2 teaspoons natural vanilla extract
200 g chopped fresh mango

Whisk the yoghurt and vanilla until smooth in a large bowl.

Process the mango in a small food processor until smooth. Fold into the yoghurt mixture to form a ripple effect.

Spoon into six ¾-cup (180 ml) ice pop moulds. Tap firmly to release any air bubbles. Insert the sticks.

Freeze for 4 hours or until set firm. Release from the moulds and serve immediately.

Family additions After releasing frozen pops from the moulds, dip in melted vegan chocolate, then roll in finely chopped toasted mixed nuts.

 Calorie booster

Add 1 teaspoon toasted chopped almonds to each mould before spooning in the mixture, or drizzle each pop with ½ teaspoon melted vegan chocolate after releasing from the mould.	30 cals

Snacks & Drinks

Afternoon booster balls

Makes
16 balls

Prep
25 minutes

Cals per serve
(per ball)
90

Vegan

When the sugar slump arrives at 3 pm, grab one of these. Packed with fibre and healthy fats, this low-cal treat will tide you over until dinner and kick those sweet cravings to the curb.

100 g flaked coconut
100 g pumpkin seeds
finely grated zest and juice of 1 lemon
2 teaspoons natural vanilla extract
2 tablespoons sugar-free drinking chocolate
1 tablespoon psyllium husk
1 tablespoon tahini

Place the coconut in a food processor and process until fine. Transfer 1/3 cup to a plate and set aside. Add the remaining ingredients to the processor, and process until the mixture comes together.

Firmly shape 1-tablespoon measures into balls, then roll lightly in the reserved coconut.

Serve or store in an airtight container in the fridge for up to 1 week.

Family additions Serve with macadamia hot chocolate.

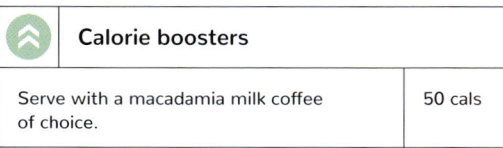

	Calorie boosters	
	Serve with a macadamia milk coffee of choice.	50 cals

Snacks & Drinks

Choc–blueberry muggy muffin

Serves 1 | Prep 10 minutes | Cook 2 minutes | Cals per serve 97 | Vegetarian

The idea of a sweet and delectable muffin being under 100 calories and taking just 2 minutes to cook seems a bit nuts, right? Well call us crazy, because we've done it! For a warm and tasty mug treat, give this one a whirl. You can thank us later.

1 egg white
1 teaspoon natural vanilla extract
3 teaspoons sugar-free drinking chocolate
1 tablespoon wholemeal plain flour
½ teaspoon baking powder
1 tablespoon frozen blueberries, plus 1 tablespoon extra

Put the egg white, vanilla and 2½ teaspoons of the drinking chocolate in a straight-sided, 1⅓ cup (330 ml) mug. Whisk with a fork until smooth.

Add the flour, baking powder and 1 tablespoon of blueberries to the mug and stir well. Sprinkle the remaining blueberries on top.

Place the mug in the centre of the microwave plate. Microwave on High for 2 minutes until cooked, puffed and the top springs back when touched – if not yet cooked, cook on High in 30-second intervals until done.

Sprinkle with the remaining drinking chocolate and serve hot.

Family additions Serve with ice cream, chocolate sauce and toasted chopped pecans.

	Calorie booster	
	Serve with a small scoop of ice cream.	130 cals

Snacks & Drinks

Macadamia chai

Serves 1   Prep 10 minutes + 3 minutes standing   Cook 10 minutes   Cals per serve 55   Vegan

This spiced bevvy is fragrantly mouth-watering, and we think it's best paired with the Choc-blueberry muggy muffin on page 211 for afternoon tea or post dinner ... but that's just us.

tea leaves from 3 tea bags
4 whole cardamom pods, bruised
4 whole cloves
¼ teaspoon cracked black pepper
¼ teaspoon ground cinnamon, plus extra to serve
½ teaspoon ground ginger
¼ teaspoon grated nutmeg, plus extra to serve
1 cup (250 ml) unsweetened macadamia milk

Combine all the ingredients in a small saucepan over low heat. Cook, stirring occasionally, for 10 minutes. Remove from the heat and leave for 3 minutes to steep. Strain into a mug and serve warm, sprinkled with extra cinnamon and nutmeg.

Family additions Sweeten with pure maple syrup and serve with biscuits.

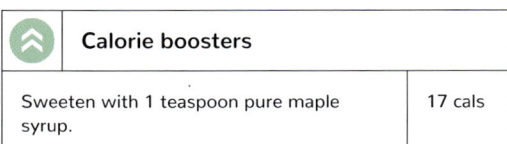

Calorie boosters	
Sweeten with 1 teaspoon pure maple syrup.	17 cals

Snacks & Drinks

Raspberry lassi

Serves 1   Prep 10 minutes   Cals per serve 96   Vegan

Lassi (not to be confused with the famous dog) is an ancient yoghurt-based smoothie, originating from the Indian subcontinent. It is a sweet, satisfying and oh-so-tasty treat to enjoy as an afternoon pick-me-up.

⅓ cup frozen raspberries
½ teaspoon finely grated lime zest
2 tablespoons natural coconut yoghurt
powdered stevia (optional), to taste
½ cup small ice cubes

Place the ingredients in a blender and process until smooth. Serve immediately.

Family additions Replace the stevia with pure maple syrup to taste, add extra raspberries and coconut yoghurt, and serve topped with toasted shredded coconut and toasted slivered almonds.

Calorie boosters

Sprinkle with 1 teaspoon toasted shredded coconut or 1 teaspoon toasted slivered almonds.	20 cals
	20 cals

Snacks & Drinks

Crazy–yum caramel frappe

Serves 1 | Prep 10 minutes | Cals per serve 95 | Vegan

Instead of forgoing hundreds of calories on gourmet flavoured coffees, give this creamy, low-cal caramel frappe a try. The foamy coffee blend is so simple and so tasty, you'll be an expert barista in no time.

¼ cup (60 ml) freshly brewed espresso
1 cup small ice cubes
1 teaspoon natural vanilla extract
1 large fresh medjool date, pitted and torn
¾ cup (180 ml) unsweetened almond milk

Place the ingredients in a blender and blend until smooth. Serve immediately.

Family additions Blend with extra dates and vegan ice cream, and sprinkle with toasted flaked almonds.

 Calorie booster

| Blend with an extra medjool date or add | 67 cals |
| 2 tablespoons vegan (or regular) ice cream. | 60 cals |

The 3-Day Diet

100
CALORIE

DESSERTS

Desserts

Choc-chip cookie and banana ice-cream sandwiches

Serves	Prep	Freezing	Cook	Cals per serve	Vegetarian
6	20 minutes	2 hours	20 minutes + cooling	(2 cookies per sandwich) 99	

Who knew something so 'naughty' could ever be this healthy? Fibre- and flavour-full are the best ways to describe these sweet treats! Go and enjoy, cheeky monkey.

2 large very ripe bananas
¾ cup (85 g) quick oats
½ teaspoon ground cinnamon
1 teaspoon pure maple syrup
2 tablespoons sugar-free dark chocolate baking chips

Slice one banana and place in a single layer on a tray lined with non-stick baking paper. Freeze for 2 hours, or until firm.

Meanwhile, preheat the oven to 180°C (160°C fan-forced). Line a large baking tray with non-stick baking paper.

Mash the remaining banana in a bowl. Stir in the oats, cinnamon, maple syrup and choc chips until well combined. Spoon 1 tablespoon of the mixture onto the lined tray and shape into a neat 5 cm round. Shape the rest of the mixture to make 12 rounds.

Bake for 18–20 minutes until cooked and golden. Cool the cookies completely on the tray.

Blend the frozen banana in a small food processor until completely smooth and creamy. Sandwich between two cookies and serve immediately.

Notes

- These cookies don't spread during baking so it's important to shape them into nice flat rounds so they cook evenly.
- The 5 cm cookies will have a chewy centre. If you prefer a crisp cookie, then flatten into 7 cm rounds and bake for 16–18 minutes, or until golden and crisp.
- 1 large overripe banana = ¾ cup mash.

Desserts

Festive vegan lemon cheesecake meringues

Makes 12   **Prep** 45 minutes   **Cook** 1 hour 15 minutes + 4 hours chilling + 4 hours drying   **Cals per serve** 92   **Vegan**

Ever wondered about the liquid in a can of chickpeas? No? Well... you should! Turns out it whips up a gorgeous vegan dessert. Head to pages 134, 138 or 142 to use the chickpeas.

400 g can chickpeas
½ cup (110 g) caster sugar
1 tablespoon cornflour
125 g vegan cream cheese
½ cup (125 g) natural coconut yoghurt
1 teaspoon natural vanilla extract
finely grated zest of 1 large lemon
125 g blueberries

Drain the chickpeas, keeping the liquid from the can (aquafaba). You will have around ⅓ cup of aquafaba. Cover and chill the aquafaba for at least 4 hours, or overnight if you have time. You will not be using the chickpeas, so put them in an airtight container in the fridge and use in another recipe.

Preheat the oven to 150°C (130°C fan-forced). Line two large baking trays with non-stick baking paper.

Transfer the chilled aquafaba to a large bowl. Beat with an electric mixer on high speed for 4–6 minutes until quadrupled in size, white and with soft peaks. Add the caster sugar, 1 tablespoon at a time, beating until dissolved before adding the next tablespoon. Use a large metal spoon to fold in the cornflour until just combined.

Spoon the mixture onto the baking trays in 12 mounds (around 2 heaped tablespoons of mixture for each mound). Leave plenty of space for spreading around each mound. Gently spread each mound to around 8 cm in diameter. Place the trays in the oven and immediately reduce the heat to 100°C (80°C fan-forced). Bake for 1 hour 15 minutes. Then turn off the oven and leave the trays inside, door closed, for at least 4 hours for the meringues to dry out.

Whisk together the cream cheese, yoghurt, vanilla and lemon zest until smooth. Spoon onto the meringues and sprinkle with blueberries to serve.

Note
- Leftover meringues can be stored in an airtight container in your pantry for up to 3 days. Leftover cheesecake mixture can be kept in an airtight container in the fridge for up to 3 days.

Yoghurt panna cotta with saffron oranges

Serves	Prep	Cook	Cals per serve	Vegetarian
4	20 mins + 4 hours chilling	10 minutes	94	

Transport yourself to the city of Roma, as you savour this zesty panna cotta. We adore how sensational this dish is, and just how fancy it looks without the effort! Bellissima!

- 4 small naval oranges, skin and white pith removed, sliced into rounds
- small pinch of saffron threads
- 2 small gelatine leaves
- 150 ml reduced-fat milk
- 1 vanilla bean, split lengthways, seeds scraped
- 1 teaspoon honey
- 4 cardamom pods, bruised
- 170 g non-fat plain Greek yoghurt

Combine the orange slices and saffron in a small bowl. Cover and chill, stirring occasionally, until ready to serve.

Soak the gelatine leaves in a bowl of water to soften.

Meanwhile, put the milk, vanilla seeds and pod, honey and cardamom in a small saucepan over medium–low heat. Cook, stirring constantly, until just before it comes to the boil. Remove from the heat.

Drain the gelatine leaves, then gently squeeze to remove excess water. Add to the milk mixture in the pan, stirring until the gelatine dissolves. Strain into a bowl, discarding the vanilla and cardamom pods. Leave to cool to room temperature.

Whisk the yoghurt into the cooled milk mixture until very smooth. Pour equally into four small ⅔ cup (160 ml) ramekins or moulds (the mixture will only three-quarters fill the ramekins). Tap the bases firmly to release and pop any air bubbles. Cover and chill for at least 4 hours.

Release the edge of each panna cotta with the tip of a small sharp knife, then turn out onto serving plates. Serve with the saffron oranges.

Choc–almond freezer fudge

Makes
26 pieces
(13 serves)

Prep
20 minutes

Freezing
30 minutes

Cals per serve
(2 pieces)
82

Vegetarian

Language warning We are fudging obsessed with these simple treats, filled with healthy fats and chocolatey goodness. These fudgers will keep for up to 1 month in the freezer.

½ cup (120 g) almond spread
½ large avocado
2 teaspoons natural vanilla extract
1 tablespoon coconut oil
¼ cup sugar-free drinking chocolate

Put all the ingredients in a small food processor and mix only until combined – take care not to overmix or the almond spread will separate.

Place 2 level teaspoons of mixture into each hole of an ice-cube tray. Press with your fingertips to flatten.

Cover with cling film and freeze for 30 minutes, or until set firm. Serve chilled or keep in the freezer for up to 1 month.

Desserts

Choc–peanut raspberry indulgence

Makes 24 | Prep 30 minutes + 4 hours chilling | Cook 5 minutes | Cals per serve 84 | Vegetarian

These delicious bites may be small, but they are mighty. Thanks to the healthy fats found in the peanut butter and coconut oil, they are sure to keep you fuller for longer.

1 cup (170 g) sugar-free dark chocolate baking chips
½ cup (140 g) smooth peanut butter
2 tablespoons coconut oil
125 g raspberries, torn in half
flaked sea salt (optional)

Line a 24-hole, 1 tablespoon-capacity mini-muffin tray with paper cases.

Stir the chocolate chips in a small heatproof bowl over a small saucepan of simmering water until melted and smooth. Spoon 1 teaspoon of melted chocolate into each muffin case, spreading to cover the base evenly.

Whisk together the peanut butter and coconut oil, then spoon evenly into the muffin cases. Top with the raspberries and a sprinkle of flaked sea salt (if using).

Chill for at least 4 hours until set firm. Serve chilled.

Note

- These can be stored in an airtight container in the fridge for up to 2 weeks.

Melon carpaccio with coconut–lime syrup

Serves 4   **Prep** 20 minutes + cooling   **Cook** 10 minutes   **Cals per serve** 85   **Vegan**

Make it summer every day with this sensational melon carpaccio. Drizzling the zesty coconut–lime syrup over the top absolutely makes this dish pop with a whole lot of fragrance and flavour. We'll meet you by the pool?

200 g peeled watermelon
200 g peeled rock melon
200 g peeled honeydew melon
2 teaspoons toasted pumpkin seeds, chopped
micro herbs (basil, coriander), to serve

Coconut–lime syrup
6 kaffir lime leaves, shredded
½ cinnamon stick
2 teaspoons honey
2 tablespoons reduced-fat coconut cream

Make the Coconut–lime syrup by placing the lime leaves, cinnamon stick, honey and 1 cup (250 ml) water in a small saucepan over high heat. Stir until the honey dissolves, then boil for 8–10 minutes, without stirring, or until reduced by half and thickened. Leave to cool to room temperature, then whisk in the coconut cream. Strain, discarding the lime leaves and cinnamon stick, and set aside.

Meanwhile, using a very sharp large knife or mandoline, shave the melon into the thinnest slices you can. Arrange on serving plates, fanning out and overlapping decoratively to cover the plates.

Drizzle the syrup over the melon. Sprinkle with the pumpkin seeds and micro herbs to serve.

Rhubarb and berry parfaits

Serves 6 | **Prep** 10 minutes + 10 minutes cooling | **Cook** 5 minutes | **Cals per serve** 93 | **Vegetarian**

How par-fect do these parfaits sound? Berry-licious and oh so simple to whip up for a fancy dessert with friends (or a simple night in with Netflix). Give these sweeties a go.

- 250 g blueberries
- 250 g raspberries
- 1 bunch rhubarb, cut into 3 cm lengths
- ½ teaspoon mixed spice
- ½ cup non-fat plain Greek yoghurt
- 2 tablespoons toasted mixed seeds, chopped
- 1 tablespoon toasted slivered almonds, chopped

Put the blueberries, raspberries, rhubarb, mixed spice and ½ cup (125 ml) water in a saucepan over medium heat. Cook, stirring occasionally, for 5 minutes or until the fruit has just collapsed and the liquid reduced by two-thirds. Cool for 10 minutes in the pan.

Spoon the warm berry mixture into six 300 ml serving glasses. Top with the yoghurt, then sprinkle with the mixed seeds and almonds. Serve immediately.

Desserts

Mini passionfruit cakes

Makes	Prep	Cook	Cals per serve	Vegan
72 (18 serves)	15 minutes	20 minutes + cooling	(4 mini cakes) 88	

We are PASSION-ate about these cutie cakes. They are so great to enjoy as an easy dessert, pop in the kids' lunchboxes or take into the office to win yourself Employee of the Week.

2 cups (300 g) self-raising flour
2 teaspoons baking powder
1 tablespoon powdered stevia
seeds scraped from 2 split vanilla beans
125 g (½ cup) unsweetened apple puree
¾ cup (180 ml) unsweetened rice milk
2 tablespoons icing sugar, sifted
pulp of 4 passionfruit

Preheat the oven to 190°C (170°C fan-forced). Line three 24-hole, 1 tablespoon-capacity mini-muffin trays with paper cases.

Whisk together the flour, baking powder, stevia and half the vanilla seeds in a large bowl. Make a well in the centre.

Stir together the apple puree, rice milk and ¼ cup (60 ml) water, then pour into the well. Fold in with a large metal spoon until sticky and just combined – do not overmix or your cakes will be tough.

Spoon the mixture evenly into the paper cases. Bake for 20 minutes, or until golden and cooked through when tested with a skewer. Leave in the trays for 3 minutes before transferring to a wire rack to cool to room temperature.

Whisk together the icing sugar, passionfruit and remaining vanilla seeds. Spoon over the cooled mini cakes to serve.

Note

- The iced mini cakes can be kept in an airtight container in the fridge for up to 3 days or wrapped into portions and frozen for up to 2 months.

FAQs

Q Are there people who shouldn't do this diet?
Yes, this diet is not recommended for the following:

- Women who are pregnant, planning to get pregnant or breastfeeding.
- Anyone with an eating disorder, a history of or a predisposition to eating disorders.
- Those with a BMI of below 20 or people who are underweight.
- Anyone who has been diagnosed with Type 1 Diabetes.
- People younger than 18 years old.
- People older than 70, without doctor's permission.

If you have any medical conditions or are taking prescription medication of any kind for any condition at all, we highly recommend speaking with your physician prior to commencing any new diet, eating or exercise regime.

Q Can I drink coffee and tea on my 'on days'?
You sure can! Black tea, black coffee and green tea all effectively contain zero calories, and they're also known to have appetite-suppressing effects. If you like to add milk, just count the calories carefully. We suggest unsweetened almond milk or oat milk over cow's milk, as they contain slightly fewer calories. (And that leaves more for wine and cheese!)

Q Do I need to worry about dehydration?
No more than you normally would, though in saying that you do get around 25 percent of your daily water intake from food, so you may need to increase your fluid intake slightly on your 'on days' to compensate for having slightly less H_2O from food. The recommended daily water intake is 2.2 litres for sedentary women and 2.7 litres for sedentary men. And remember, even mild dehydration can cause dry skin, fatigue, decreased brain function, anxiety, headaches and migraines, sugar cravings and high blood pressure! Yep, water is life alright.

Q Do I have to count calories on my days off?
We do recommend this for the best results, at least to begin with. But you don't need to walk around with a calculator. Once you start to get used to how many calories are in different foods, you'll be able to ease up on the counting.

Q Should I take a multivitamin?
Good question! Since this approach allows you a lot of freedom to choose what you eat, what you end up eating may not be as balanced as some other approaches to dieting. The recipes we've included focus on nutrient-rich foods like veggies, protein and low GI carbohydrates, so where you can, try to stick to them. Before you decide to invest in a multivitamin,

it's best to have a proper blood test from your GP, because otherwise you're just creating expensive wee.

Q Can I drink alcohol?
Where have you been for this entire book? If we could've called it The Wine and Cheese Diet, we would have. We don't recommend drinking alcohol on your 'on days', as it's quite calorie dense, and as well as increasing your appetite, it can also impair your judgement. Your body regards it as a toxin, so it will forego processing regular food calories in favour of eliminating the alcohol calories first, which means anything you eat while drinking alcohol will be stored away as fat. But on your 'off days'? One hundred percent.

Q If I exercise, can I eat the extra calories I burn?
Nope, sorry. (Nice try!) Most people vastly overestimate the number of calories they burn when they exercise. Exercise machines can miscalculate calories burned by between 50 and 100 percent. For example, the average treadmill will tell you you've burned anywhere between 300 and 400 calories in 30 minutes, when realistically, most people will only burn 100 to 200. Meaning if you do eat the extra calories, you may actually gain weight.

Q Why does my weight fluctuate over the course of a day?
Don't stress about those little daily ups and downs, they're totally normal. Body weight fluctuates by around 0.5 kg to 1.5 kg each day because of the weight of the food in your stomach, the amount of water your body retains. It can also be due to hormonal fluctuations. For the most accurate scale reading, weigh yourself at the same time on the same day each week before eating or drinking anything. As long as the scales show a consistent downward trend, you're golden.

Q How do you restart weight loss when you hit a plateau?
Plateaus are a normal part of weight loss. They tend to happen somewhere around 4 and 6 months in, when you get close to the normal weight range indicated by your BMI chart. However, this doesn't mean you can't keep losing weight. All that's required to restart your weight loss is to recalculate your metabolic rate or TDEE to take into account your smaller frame, and you're back on the fast track. Head back to page 99 for our best plateau-busting tips.

Q How long does it take to adjust to 3-day dieting?
This varies from person to person, but research shows that after about a week or so, hunger decreases and feelings of fullness increase. Specifically, on the first 3 to 5 'on days', you may feel a little tired, cold, hungry, headachey or irritable as your body adjusts to the new way of eating. It's critical not to give up during this time, as the first week or so isn't an accurate representation of what you'll feel if you persist. Week 2 is so much easier, and you'll be feeling fab before you know it. Promise!

Where to from here?

Where NOT to from here? The world is your oyster, you absolute epic legend! You've learned so much about yourself over the past few weeks and months, that there's nothing you can't do. Go forth and be fabulous, you great big spunk. We hope you'll join us on our award-winning online program, which has so much more content than we could possibly ever fit into a book.

If you want to chat with us personally, just send us an email at info@superfastdiet.com.

We truly would love to hear from you.

Don't forget, we've created a free trial link to help you smash your goals here: superfastdiet.com/3daydietbook

Downloads, sources, worksheets and printables

Jump online at superfastdiet.com/3daydietbook to find sources, recommendations for further reading, nifty worksheets and printable tools to help you get the most from the 3-day diet – and to get your BONUS Secret Chapter.

Go online And make sure you join our 3-day diet Facebook support group here: facebook.com/groups/3daydiet

Thank you

A very big SUPER ...THANK YOU! THANK YOU! THANK YOU! We cannot begin to express how grateful we are to everyone who gave their heart and soul to this brilliant book of transformation.

Firstly, to our terrific team at SuperFastDiet: our word magician and chief researcher Rosemary Slade – you are fabulous, funny and a scientific genius. What a combo! Our food goddess and recipe writer Tracey Pattison – you truly help us live our best, most delicious, nourished life. Tara Samuel, your word-wrangling and cheeky jokes are a delight. Nicola Daniels, our Head of Operations. Without you we'd be a complete mess. Jen Picknell, our Head of Making Things Pretty – you have such talent and wit. Thanks also to our incredible team, especially Vanessa Giblin, Kirsten Wenborne, Trish Gowlett, Joyce Lonzaga and Nicole Santos, plus Angie O'Reilly and our amazing super coaches.

All the Pan Macmillan stars who have made creating this book a complete joy, led by the super-professional, clever and gorgeous publisher Ingrid Ohlsson. Thank you for saying 'you had me at 3-day diet'. Additionally, your phenomenal team: Danielle Walker, Naomi van Groll, Samantha Manson and Candice Wyman, plus Katie Bosher and Jane Price, editors extraordinaire.

Also thanks to fabulous photographer Rob Palmer, super-stylist Em Knowles, shoot team James Callaway, Peta Dent and Kerrie Ray, along with designer Jacqui Porter. For our fabulous, glamorous people shots thanks to Simona Janek with hair and makeup by Miriam Van Cooten.

We are also very grateful to our contributing scientist Krista Varady, PhD, who is the global go-to guru for intermittent-fasting research and Professor of Nutrition at the University of Illinois, Chicago.

And most especially to our incredible case studies: Mary-Anne O'Connor, Viginia Fraser, Myles Haslam and Kristen Black. Not to mention a gigantic, super-duper thankyou to all our SuperFastDiet.com members for inspiring us every day with your enthusiasm and awesome transformations.

Finally, massive thanks from the bottom of our hearts to our Supermen – our hubbies, John and Paul – who, along with our families, have supported us every step of this life-changing journey.

You are all our Superheroes!
Biggest love,

Vic and Gen xo

Conversion chart

Measuring cups and spoons may vary slightly from one country to another, but the difference is generally not enough to affect a recipe. All cup and spoon measures are level. One Australian metric measuring cup holds 250 ml (8 fl oz), one Australian metric tablespoon holds 20 ml (4 teaspoons) and one Australian metric teaspoon holds 5 ml. North America, New Zealand and the UK use a 15 ml (3-teaspoon) tablespoon.

Length

METRIC	IMPERIAL
3 mm	⅛ inch
6 mm	¼ inch
1 cm	½ inch
2.5 cm	1 inch
5 cm	2 inches
18 cm	7 inches
20 cm	8 inches
23 cm	9 inches
25 cm	10 inches
30 cm	12 inches

Liquid measures

ONE AMERICAN PINT	ONE IMPERIAL PINT
500 ml (16 fl oz)	600 ml (20 fl oz)

CUP	METRIC	IMPERIAL
⅛ cup	30 ml	1 fl oz
¼ cup	60 ml	2 fl oz
⅓ cup	80 ml	2½ fl oz
½ cup	125 ml	4 fl oz
⅔ cup	160 ml	5 fl oz
¾ cup	180 ml	6 fl oz
1 cup	250 ml	8 fl oz
2 cups	500 ml	16 fl oz
2¼ cups	560 ml	20 fl oz
4 cups	1 litre	32 fl oz

Dry measures

The most accurate way to measure dry ingredients is to weigh them. However, if using a cup, add the ingredient loosely to the cup and level with a knife; don't compact the ingredient unless the recipe requests 'firmly packed'.

METRIC	IMPERIAL
15 g	½ oz
30 g	1 oz
60 g	2 oz
125 g	4 oz (¼ lb)
185 g	6 oz
250 g	8 oz (½ lb)
375 g	12 oz (¾ lb)
500 g	16 oz (1 lb)
1 kg	32 oz (2 lb)

Oven temperatures

CELSIUS	FAHRENHEIT
100°C	200°F
120°C	250°F
150°C	300°F
160°C	325°F
180°C	350°F
200°C	400°F
220°C	425°F

CELSIUS	GAS MARK
110°C	¼
130°C	½
140°C	1
150°C	2
170°C	3
180°C	4
190°C	5
200°C	6
220°C	7
230°C	8
240°C	9
250°C	10

Index

3-day diet
  adjusting to 231
  benefits 20–3
  eating out 71
  fixed/flexy approaches to eating 32–3
  getting started 37–43
  no calorie-counting approach 58–9
  on a plate 64–7
  potential pitfalls 92–8
  six habits for success 85–91
  staying on track 102–3
  story of 13–15
  supercharging method 47–51
  what is 19, 26
  who shouldn't do it 230
  see also intermittent fasting
5:2 diet 10, 14, 28
16:8 method 28, 14, 48, 103
  see also supercharging method

A
Afternoon booster balls 210
alcohol 26, 71, 78–81, 102, 231
anxiety 23, 87, 90, 230
Apple cranberry bircher 131
apples
  Apple cranberry bircher 131
  Chicken Waldorf sandwich 135
  Mini passionfruit cakes 229
apricots: Astounding apricot chicken capsicums 152
asparagus: Charming chargrilled barramundi with cauli mash and creamy lemon sauce 164
aspartame 73
Astounding apricot chicken capsicums 152
autophagy 23
avocado
  Beef and wild rice bowls 151
  Choc–almond freezer fudge 223
  Hearty but healthy turkey nachos 175
  Mexican bean and roast pumpkin salad 193
  Mexican sweet potato boats 196
  radish salad 172
  Rainbow veggie rosti with avocado, tomatoes and dukkah 126
  Sashimi sushi rolls 140
  Sesame beef and radish salad 172

B
bananas
  Choc-chip cookie and banana ice-cream sandwiches 218
  Choc–banana muffins 124
barley: Tandoori salmon and barley bowls 150
barramundi, Charming chargrilled, with cauli mash and creamy lemon sauce 164

Basic dried spice blend 113
Basic muffin recipe 124
Basic spice paste 113
Basic veggie paste 113
beans
  Beans and greens soup 139
  Beef and wild rice bowls 151
  Black bean and pulse pasta bowls 150
  Broccoli and feta frittata with crouton topping 190
  Egg and soba noodle salad 142
  Egg nicoise sandwich 135
  Green machine cannellini stew 187
  Mexican bean and roast pumpkin salad 193
  Mexican sweet potato boats 196
  Mushroom and bean goulash soup 191
  Pumpkin–chickpea patties with fab feta yoghurt 184
  Roast potato salad 144
  Roast salmon with veggie fries and SFD terrific tartare sauce 169
  Spiced chicken breast and veggie tray bake 156
Beans and greens soup 139
beef
  Beef and beetroot hummus sandwich 134
  Beef and wild rice bowls 151
  Mongolian beef with veggie noodles 183
  Peppered beef and strawberry salad 181
  Sesame beef and radish salad 172
Beef and beetroot hummus sandwich 134
Beef and wild rice bowls 151
berries see blueberries, raspberries, strawberries
bingeing 95
bircher, Apple cranberry 131
Black bean and pulse pasta bowls 150
blueberries
  Choc–blueberry muggy muffin 211
  Festive vegan lemon cheesecake meringues 220
  Ginger blueberry muffins 124
  Rhubarb and berry parfaits 228
bok choy
  Garlic chicken and quinoa bowls 149
  Slow-cooker five-spice chicken 157
bolognese, Lentil-as-anything 200
broccoli
  Broccoli and feta frittata with crouton topping 190
  Korma chickpea and freekeh bowls 148
  Slow-cooker lamb and sweet potato casserole 177
Broccoli and feta frittata with crouton topping 190

broth, Herbaceous vegetable 115
brussels sprouts
  Roast cauli, tofu and orange salad 201
  Roast veggie tofu scramble 120

C
cakes
  Festive vegan lemon cheesecake meringues 220
  Mini passionfruit cakes 229
calories 13, 14, 15, 19, 24, 48, 72
  1, 2, 3, 4 approach 56, 58–9
  adjusting to maintain weight 103
  calorie restriction 6, 28
  counting 49–50, 230
  in restaurant desserts 76–7
  intake across the day 25
  in wine 78–9
  low-calorie staples 61
  low-calorie swaps 30–1
  no calorie-counting approach 58–9
  skinny drinks 80–1
capsicum
  Astounding apricot chicken capsicums 152
  Egg and soba noodle salad 142
  Friday night flatbread pizzas 188
  Full breakfast tray bake 130
  Ham and capsicum melt toast topper 118
  Mexican bean and roast pumpkin salad 193
  Mexican sweet potato boats 196
  Mongolian beef with veggie noodles 183
  Mushroom fajita lettuce rolls 140
  Mushroom kebabs and quinoa tabbouli 194
  Prawn rice salad 143
  Prawny fried rice 163
  quinoa tabbouli 194
  Tamari chicken and veggie salad 144
  Tantalising Thai yellow fish curry 166
  Tasty tempeh tacos 197
  Tip-top tamari pork stir-fry 178
  Turmeric capsicum tofu scramble 120
carbohydrates 58
carrots
  Basic veggie paste 113
  Beef and wild rice bowls 151
  Cauli-freddo with crispy kale 199
  Curried chickpeas sandwich 134
  Curried-egg mountain bread roll 140
  Fancy filo-topped salmon pie 171
  Hearty veggie and chicken soup 138
  Herbaceous vegetable broth 115
  Lentil-as-anything bolognese 200
  Mongolian beef with veggie noodles 183

Prawn rice salad 143
radish salad 172
Rainbow veggie rosti with avocado, tomatoes and dukkah 126
Roast pumpkin dip 204
Roast salmon with veggie fries and SFD terrific tartare sauce 169
Sesame beef and radish salad 172
Spiced carrot and cauliflower soup 138
Vegelicious tomato sauce 114
casserole, Slow-cooker lamb and sweet potato 177
cauliflower
Cauli-freddo with crispy kale 199
Charming chargrilled barramundi with cauli mash and creamy lemon sauce 164
Prawny fried rice 163
Roast cauli, tofu and orange salad 201
Slow-cooker lamb and sweet potato casserole 177
Spiced carrot and cauliflower soup 138
Cauli-freddo with crispy kale 199
celery
Basic veggie paste 113
Chicken Waldorf sandwich 135
Egg and soba noodle salad 142
Fancy filo-topped salmon pie 171
Hearty zucchini, kale and quinoa soup 138
Herbaceous vegetable broth 115
Mexican bean and roast pumpkin salad 193
Tofu couscous salad 144
Tuna and veggie macaroni bake 170
Vegelicious tomato sauce 114
chai, Macadamia 212
Chargrilled pork and grape salad 176
Charming chargrilled barramundi with cauli mash and creamy lemon sauce 164
cheese
Chicken Caesar mountain bread roll 140
Full breakfast tray bake 130
Ham and capsicum melt toast topper 118
Tuna and veggie macaroni bake 170
Zucchini salsa melts 207
see also feta, ricotta
chicken
Astounding apricot chicken capsicums 152
Chicken and spinach dahl 155
Chicken Caesar mountain bread roll 140
Chicken Waldorf sandwich 135
Curried chicken and mango magic salad 161
Garlic chicken and quinoa bowls 149
Greek chicken meatballs and Zeus salad 160
Hearty veggie and chicken soup 138
Impossible chicken, feta and chive quiche 158
Slow-cooker five-spice chicken 157

Spiced chicken breast and veggie tray bake 156
Tamari chicken and veggie salad 144
Chicken and spinach dahl 155
Chicken Caesar mountain bread roll 140
Chicken Waldorf sandwich 135
chickpeas
Creamy pumpkin with crunchy cumin chickpeas soup 138
Curried chickpeas sandwich 134
Deconstructed falafel salad 142
Festive vegan lemon cheesecake meringues 220
Korma chickpea and freekeh bowls 148
Pumpkin–chickpea patties with fab feta yoghurt 184
chillies
Basic spice paste 113
Sweet chilli prawns with crunchy noodle salad 162
Choc-chip cookie and banana ice-cream sandwiches 218
Choc–almond freezer fudge 223
Choc–banana muffins 124
Choc–blueberry muggy muffin 211
Choc–peanut raspberry indulgence 224
chocolate
Afternoon booster balls 210
Choc-chip cookie and banana ice-cream sandwiches 218
Choc–almond freezer fudge 223
Choc–banana muffins 124
Choc–blueberry muggy muffin 211
Choc–peanut raspberry indulgence 224
cholesterol 22, 87
HDL and LDL cholesterol 22, 48
coconut: Afternoon booster balls 210
coconut–lime syrup 227
coffee 49, 50, 51, 100, 230
Crazy–yum caramel frappe 215
comfort eating 95
cookie, Choc-chip, and banana ice-cream sandwiches 218
corn
Mexican sweet potato boats 196
Prawny fried rice 163
Slow-cooker five-spice chicken 157
Tamari chicken and veggie salad 144
cortisol 88, 89, 102
couscous
Astounding apricot chicken capsicums 152
Moroccan pumpkin and couscous bowls 148
Tofu couscous salad 144
cravings 6, 22, 29, 55, 88
snacks for 74–5
sugar cravings 72–3, 230
Crazy–yum caramel frappe 215
Creamy dollop 112
creamy lemon sauce 164
Creamy pumpkin with crunchy cumin chickpeas soup 138
crunchy noodle salad 162

cucumbers
Beef and beetroot hummus sandwich 134
crunchy noodle salad 162
Curried chicken and mango magic salad 161
Deconstructed falafel salad 142
Mushroom kebabs and quinoa tabbouli 194
Peppered beef and strawberry salad 181
quinoa tabbouli 194
Salmon and nutty cream cheese sandwich 134
strawberry salad 181
Sweet chilli prawns with crunchy noodle salad 162
Tandoori salmon and barley bowls 150
Tasty tempeh tacos 197
Tofu couscous salad 144
Curried chicken and mango magic salad 161
Curried chickpeas sandwich 134
Curried-egg mountain bread roll 140
curry, Tantalising Thai yellow fish 166

D
dahl, Chicken and spinach 155
dates
Crazy–yum caramel frappe 215
Divine dates with lime ricotta 206
Deconstructed falafel salad 142
dehydration 230
depression 23, 87, 90, 100
desserts, restaurant 76–7
diets 6, 8–11, 13, 14, 27
5:2 diet 10, 14, 28
SuperFastDiet 8–11, 13, 15, 24, 85, 93, 232
see also 3-day diet, 16:8 method
dip: Roast pumpkin dip 204
Divine dates with lime ricotta 206
dressings 112
drinks, skinny 80–1
drizzle, Tamari–ginger 112

E
eating out 71, 76–7
Egg and soba noodle salad 142
Egg nicoise sandwich 135
eggplant: Friday night flatbread pizzas 188
eggs
Broccoli and feta frittata with crouton topping 190
Curried-egg mountain bread roll 140
Egg and soba noodle salad 142
Egg nicoise sandwich 135
Full breakfast tray bake 130
Garlic mushroom and pea egg scramble 120
Herb and tomato omelette toast topper 119
Impossible chicken, feta and chive quiche 158

Prawny fried rice 163
Tomato and mushroom egg scramble 120
Tuna omelette roll 140
Zucchini and kale egg scramble 120
energy, total daily, expenditure (TDEE) 24, 25, 49, 99, 231
exercise 6, 19, 29, 87, 99, 102, 103, 231

F
Fancy filo-topped salmon pie 171
fast food options 97
fasting
 alternate daily fasting (ADF) 14
 see also intermittent fasting, time-restricted eating
fat burning 15, 20, 27, 29, 47, 48
fennel
 Green machine cannellini stew 187
 Hearty veggie and chicken soup 138
Festive vegan lemon cheesecake meringues 220
feta
 Broccoli and feta frittata with crouton topping 190
 Friday night flatbread pizzas 188
 Greek chicken meatballs and Zeus salad 160
 Ham, corn and feta muffins 125
 Hummus, tomato and feta toast topper 119
 Impossible chicken, feta and chive quiche 158
 Pumpkin–chickpea patties with fab feta yoghurt 184
fish
 Charming chargrilled barramundi with cauli mash and creamy lemon sauce 164
 Tantalising Thai yellow fish curry 166
 see also salmon, tuna
food
 comfort eating 95
 food swaps 30–1
 macronutrients 56
 meal prepping tips and tricks 62–3
frappe, Crazy–yum caramel 215
freekeh: Korma chickpea and freekeh bowls 148
Friday night flatbread pizzas 188
fried rice, Prawny 163
frittata, Broccoli and feta, with crouton topping 190
fudge, Choc–almond freezer 223
Full breakfast tray bake 130

G
Garlic chicken and quinoa bowls 149
Garlic mushroom and pea egg scramble 120
Ginger blueberry muffins 124
Gluten-free muesli 114
Gluten-free muesli and raspberry parfaits 129

goal setting 37, 40–1, 99
grapes: Chargrilled pork and grape salad 176
Greek chicken meatballs and Zeus salad 160
green beans see beans
Green machine cannellini stew 187

H
habits 92
Ham and capsicum melt toast topper 118
Ham, corn and feta muffins 125
happiness 88, 90
HDL cholesterol 22, 48
Hearty but healthy turkey nachos 175
Hearty veggie and chicken soup 138
Hearty zucchini, kale and quinoa soup 138
Herb and tomato omelette toast topper 119
Herb-crumbed lamb cutlets and slaw 182
Herbaceous vegetable broth 115
Hummus, tomato and feta toast topper 119

I
ice-cream sandwiches, Choc-chip cookie and banana 218
Impossible chicken, feta and chive quiche 158
intermittent fasting 10–11, 13–15, 19, 21, 22–3, 27–8, 47, 48, 49–51, 99
 adjusting methods to maintain weight 103
 see also 3-day diet, 5:2 diet, 16:8 method, time-restricted eating

K
kale
 Black bean and pulse pasta bowls 150
 Cauli-freddo with crispy kale 199
 Hearty zucchini, kale and quinoa soup 138
 Zucchini and kale egg scramble 120
ketosis 20, 47, 51
Korma chickpea and freekeh bowls 148

L
lamb
 Herb-crumbed lamb cutlets and slaw 182
 Slow-cooker lamb and sweet potato casserole 177
lassi, Raspberry 214
LDL cholesterol 22, 48
Lemon poppy seed muffins 125
Lemon–pepper ricotta and salmon toast topper 118
lemons
 Afternoon booster balls 210
 Creamy dollop 112
 creamy lemon sauce 164
 Festive vegan lemon cheesecake meringues 220

Greek chicken meatballs and Zeus salad 160
Hearty zucchini, kale and quinoa soup 138
Lemon poppy seed muffins 125
Lemon–pepper ricotta and salmon toast topper 118
Roast pumpkin dip 204
Roast salmon with veggie fries and SFD terrific tartare sauce 169
Salmon and nutty cream cheese sandwich 134
Virtually no-cal-gal dressing 112
Zucchini and kale egg scramble 120
Lentil-as-anything bolognese 200
lentils
 Chicken and spinach dahl 155
 Lentil-as-anything bolognese 200
leptin 72, 89
limes
 Beef and wild rice bowls 151
 Chicken and spinach dahl 155
 Curried chicken and mango magic salad 161
 Divine dates with lime ricotta 206
 Hearty but healthy turkey nachos 175
 Prawn tom yum soup 139
 Raspberry lassi 214
 Tamari–ginger drizzle 112
 Tip-top tamari pork stir-fry 178

M
Macadamia chai 212
Mango fro-yo pops 209
mangos
 Curried chicken and mango magic salad 161
 Mango fro-yo pops 209
Marinated mushrooms toast topper 119
meatballs, Greek chicken, and Zeus salad 160
Melon carpaccio with coconut–lime syrup 227
menopause 20
metabolism 6, 20, 27, 48
Mexican bean and roast pumpkin salad 193
Mexican sweet potato boats 196
mindset
 positive self-talk 86–7
 six habits of successful slimmers 85–91
 potential pitfalls 92–9
Mini passionfruit cakes 229
Mongolian beef with veggie noodles 183
mood
 10 super-good-mood foods 100
 funky feels 98
Moroccan pumpkin and couscous bowls 148
muesli
 Gluten-free muesli 114
 Gluten-free muesli and raspberry parfaits 129
muffins 124–25, 211

multivitamins 230
Mushroom and bean goulash soup 191
Mushroom fajita lettuce rolls 140
Mushroom kebabs and quinoa
    tabbouli 194
mushrooms
    Garlic mushroom and pea egg
        scramble 120
    Marinated mushrooms toast topper 119
    Mushroom and bean goulash soup 191
    Mushroom fajita lettuce rolls 140
    Mushroom kebabs and quinoa
        tabbouli 194
    Tomato and mushroom egg
        scramble 120

N
nachos, Hearty but healthy turkey 175
noodles: Egg and soba noodle salad 142
olives: Greek chicken meatballs and Zeus
    salad 160
omelette, Herb and tomato, toast
    topper 119
oranges
    Roast cauli, tofu and orange salad 201
    Tofu couscous salad 144
    Yoghurt panna cotta with saffron
        oranges 221

P
panna cotta, Yoghurt, with saffron
    oranges 221
parfait
    Gluten-free muesli and raspberry
        parfaits 129
    Rhubarb and berry parfaits 228
part-time dieting 19, 22, 27, 47
passionfruit: Mini passionfruit cakes 229
pasta
    Black bean and pulse pasta bowls 150
    Green machine cannellini stew 187
    Lentil-as-anything bolognese 200
    Tuna and veggie macaroni bake 170
pastes 113
patties, Pumpkin–chickpea, with fab feta
    yoghurt 184
peas
    Curried-egg mountain bread roll 140
    Garlic chicken and quinoa bowls 149
    Garlic mushroom and pea egg
        scramble 120
    Prawn tom yum soup 139
    Prawny fried rice 163
    Tantalising Thai yellow fish curry 166
    Tip-top tamari pork stir-fry 178
Peppered beef and strawberry salad 181
pie, Fancy filo-topped salmon 171
pizzas, Friday night flatbread 188
pork
    Chargrilled pork and grape salad 176
    Full breakfast tray bake 130
    Ham and capsicum melt toast
        topper 118
    Ham, corn and feta muffins 125

Tip-top tamari pork stir-fry 178
positive self-talk 86–7
potatoes
    Charming chargrilled barramundi
        with cauli mash and creamy lemon
        sauce 164
    Mushroom and bean goulash soup 191
    Roast potato salad 144
    Spiced chicken breast and veggie tray
        bake 156
    Prawn cocktail sandwich 135
    Prawn rice salad 143
    Prawn tom yum soup 139
prawns
    Prawn cocktail sandwich 135
    Prawn rice salad 143
    Prawn tom yum soup 139
    Prawny fried rice 163
    Sweet chilli prawns with crunchy
        noodle salad 162
Prawny fried rice 163
pumpkin
    Creamy pumpkin with crunchy cumin
        chickpeas soup 138
    Full breakfast tray bake 130
    Hearty veggie and chicken soup 138
    Mexican bean and roast pumpkin
        salad 193
    Moroccan pumpkin and couscous
        bowls 148
    Pumpkin–chickpea patties with fab feta
        yoghurt 184
    Rainbow veggie rosti with avocado,
        tomatoes and dukkah 126
    Roast potato salad 144
    Roast pumpkin dip 204
    Roast veggie tofu scramble 120
    Tantalising Thai yellow fish curry 166
    Tuna and veggie macaroni bake 170
Pumpkin–chickpea patties with fab feta
    yoghurt 184

Q
quiche, Impossible chicken, feta and
    chive 158
quinoa
    Garlic chicken and quinoa bowls 149
    Hearty zucchini, kale and quinoa
        soup 138
    Mushroom kebabs and quinoa
        tabbouli 194

R
radish salad 172
radishes
    Chargrilled pork and grape salad 176
    Curried chicken and mango magic
        salad 161
    radish salad 172
    Roast pumpkin dip 204
    Sesame beef and radish salad 172
    Tofu couscous salad 144
    Rainbow veggie rosti with avocado,
        tomatoes and dukkah 126

raspberries
    Choc–peanut raspberry indulgence
        224
    Gluten-free muesli and raspberry
        parfaits 129
    Raspberry cheesecake ripple
        muffins 125
    Raspberry lassi 214
    Rhubarb and berry parfaits 228
Raspberry cheesecake ripple muffins 125
Raspberry lassi 214
rest 88–9
Rhubarb and berry parfaits 228
rice
    Beef and wild rice bowls 151
    Prawn rice salad 143
    Tip-top tamari pork stir-fry 178
Rice paper tofu rolls 140
ricotta
    Divine dates with lime ricotta 206
    Lemon–pepper ricotta and salmon
        toast topper 118
Ricotta spinach muffins 125
Ricotta spinach muffins 125
Roast cauli, tofu and orange salad 201
Roast potato salad 144
Roast pumpkin dip 204
Roast salmon with veggie fries and SFD
    terrific tartare sauce 169
Roast veggie tofu scramble 120
rolls that rock 140–1
rosti, Rainbow veggie, with avocado,
    tomatoes and dukkah 126

S
salads
    Chargrilled pork and grape salad 176
    crunchy noodle salad 162
    Curried chicken and mango magic
        salad 161
    Deconstructed falafel salad 142
    Egg and soba noodle salad 142
    Greek chicken meatballs and Zeus
        salad 160
    make-ahead 142–5
    Mexican bean and roast pumpkin
        salad 193
    Peppered beef and strawberry
        salad 181
    Prawn rice salad 143
    quinoa tabbouli 194
    radish salad 172
    Roast cauli, tofu and orange salad 201
    Roast potato salad 144
    Sesame beef and radish salad 172
    strawberry salad 181
    Sweet chilli prawns with crunchy
        noodle salad 162
    Tamari chicken and veggie salad 144
    Tofu couscous salad 144
salmon
    Fancy filo-topped salmon pie 171
    Lemon–pepper ricotta and salmon
        toast topper 118

Roast salmon with veggie fries and SFD terrific tartare sauce 169
Salmon and nutty cream cheese sandwich 134
Sashimi sushi rolls 140
Tandoori salmon and barley bowls 150
Salmon and nutty cream cheese sandwich 134
sandwiches 134–35
Sashimi sushi rolls 140
sauces
  creamy lemon sauce 164
  SFD tartare sauce 169
  Vegelicious tomato sauce 114
self-sabotage 94
Sesame beef and radish salad 172
SFD tartare sauce 169
silverbeet
  Beans and greens soup 139
  Lentil-as-anything bolognese 200
sleep 88–9, 102
  and appetite 89
Slow-cooker five-spice chicken 157
Slow-cooker lamb and sweet potato casserole 177
snacks 74–5
soups
  Beans and greens soup 139
  Creamy pumpkin with crunchy cumin chickpeas soup 138
  Hearty veggie and chicken soup 138
  Hearty zucchini, kale and quinoa soup 138
  Mushroom and bean goulash soup 191
  Prawn tom yum soup 139
  Spiced carrot and cauliflower soup 138
spice blends 113
Spiced carrot and cauliflower soup 138
Spiced chicken breast and veggie tray bake 156
spinach
  Chicken and spinach dahl 155
  Korma chickpea and freekeh bowls 148
  Marinated mushrooms toast topper 119
  Prawn tom yum soup 139
  radish salad 172
  Ricotta spinach muffins 125
  Salmon and nutty cream cheese sandwich 134
  Sesame beef and radish salad 172
  Slow-cooker lamb and sweet potato casserole 177
  Tandoori salmon and barley bowls 150
  Tuna omelette roll 140
squash
  Chargrilled pork and grape salad 176
  Green machine cannellini stew 187
stews: Green machine cannellini stew 187
stir-fry, Tip-top tamari pork 178
strawberry salad 181
stress 23, 87, 88, 90, 102
styling 90–1
sugar 72–3
  in wine 78–9

substitutes 73
supercharging method 47–51
SuperFastDiet 8–11, 13, 15, 24, 85, 93, 232
  see also 3-day diet
sushi rolls, Sashimi 140
Sweet chilli prawns with crunchy noodle salad 162
sweet potatoes
  Mexican sweet potato boats 196
  Roast salmon with veggie fries and SFD terrific tartare sauce 169
  Slow-cooker lamb and sweet potato casserole 177
syrup, coconut–lime 227

T
tabbouli, quinoa 194
tacos, Tasty tempeh 197
Tamari chicken and veggie salad 144
Tamari–ginger drizzle 112
Tandoori salmon and barley bowls 150
Tantalising Thai yellow fish curry 166
tartare sauce, SFD 169
Tasty tempeh tacos 197
tea 49, 50, 51, 230
tempeh: Tasty tempeh tacos 197
Thyme-ly mustard dressing 112
time-restricted eating 14, 48
  see also 16:8 diet
Tip-top tamari pork stir-fry 178
toast toppers, filling 118–19
tofu
  Rice paper tofu rolls 140
  Roast cauli, tofu and orange salad 201
  Roast veggie tofu scramble 120
  Tofu couscous salad 144
  Turmeric capsicum tofu scramble 120
Tofu couscous salad 144
Tomato and mushroom egg scramble 120
tomatoes
  Chicken Caesar mountain bread roll 140
  Deconstructed falafel salad 142
  Friday night flatbread pizzas 188
  Full breakfast tray bake 130
  Greek chicken meatballs and Zeus salad 160
  Herb and tomato omelette toast topper 119
  Herbaceous vegetable broth 115
  Hummus, tomato and feta toast topper 119
  Prawn tom yum soup 139
  Rainbow veggie rosti with avocado, tomatoes and dukkah 126
  Spiced chicken breast and veggie tray bake 156
  Tomato and mushroom egg scramble 120
  Vegelicious tomato sauce 114
total daily energy expenditure (TDEE) 24, 25, 49, 99, 231
Tuna and veggie macaroni bake 170
Tuna omelette roll 140

turkey: Hearty but healthy turkey nachos 175
Turmeric capsicum tofu scramble 120

V
Vegelicious tomato sauce 114
Virtually no-cal-gal dressing 112
visualisation 42–3

W
watermelon *see* melon
weight loss 6–7, 8–11, 13–15, 19, 20–1, 26, 27, 29, 48, 88
  facing the scales 38–9
  maintaining 103
  plateau 99, 231
  supercharging method 47–51
  the last three-to-five kilos 102
  toolkit 43
wine 78–9

Y
Yoghurt panna cotta with saffron oranges 221

Z
zucchini
  Basic veggie paste 113
  Cauli-freddo with crispy kale 199
  Creamy pumpkin with crunchy cumin chickpeas soup 138
  crunchy noodle salad 162
  Full breakfast tray bake 130
  Green machine cannellini stew 187
  Hearty veggie and chicken soup 138
  Hearty zucchini, kale and quinoa soup 138
  Herbaceous vegetable broth 115
  Lentil-as-anything bolognese 200
  Mongolian beef with veggie noodles 183
  Moroccan pumpkin and couscous bowls 148
  Pumpkin–chickpea patties with fab feta yoghurt 184
  Rainbow veggie rosti with avocado, tomatoes and dukkah 126
  Roast salmon with veggie fries and SFD terrific tartare sauce 169
  Sweet chilli prawns with crunchy noodle salad 162
  Tamari chicken and veggie salad 144
  Tasty tempeh tacos 197
  Tuna and veggie macaroni bake 170
  Vegelicious tomato sauce 114
  Zucchini and kale egg scramble 120
  Zucchini salsa melts 207
Zucchini and kale egg scramble 120
Zucchini salsa melts 207

First published 2021 in Macmillan by Pan Macmillan Australia Pty Limited
Level 25, 1 Market Street, Sydney, New South Wales, Australia 2000

Text copyright © Victoria Black and Gen Davidson 2021
Photographs Rob Palmer copyright © Pan Macmillan 2021
Portrait photography by Simona Janek, with hair and makeup by Miriam Van Cooten
Image on page 40 © iStock; pages 57 and 73 © Shutterstock;
pages 80-81 © Daria Arnautova / Alamy Stock Photo and Shutterstock;
pages 100-101 © Shutterstock; page 116 Yashaswita Bhoir / Unsplash

The moral right of the author to be identified as the author of this work has been asserted.

All rights reserved. No part of this book may be reproduced or transmitted by any person or entity (including Google, Amazon or similar organisations), in any form or by any means, electronic or mechanical, including photocopying, recording, scanning or by any information storage and retrieval system, without prior permission in writing from the publisher. The author and the publisher have made every effort to contact copyright holders for material used in this book. Any person or organisation that may have been overlooked should contact the publisher.

 A catalogue record for this book is available from the National Library of Australia

Design by Northwood Green
Recipe development by Tracey Pattison
Edited by Katie Bosher and Jane Price
Indexing by Helena Holmgren
Prop and food styling by Emma Knowles
Food preparation by James Callaway, Peta Dent and Kerrie Ray
Colour + reproduction by Splitting Image Colour Studio
Printed in China by 1010 Printing International Limited

We advise that the information contained in this book does not negate personal responsibility on the part of the reader for their own health and safety. It is recommended that individually tailored advice is sought from your healthcare or medical professional. The publishers and their respective employees, agents and authors are not liable for injuries or damage occasioned to any person as a result of reading or following the information contained in this book.

10 9 8 7 6 5 4 3 2 1